One Life to Live:

How Letting Go Leads to a Life That Counts

Devin Dummel

One Life to Live
Copyright @ 2019 by Devin Dummel

Requests for information should be addressed to:
High Five Publishing, 10876 Spirit Dr., Ingalls, IN 46048

ISBN 978-1-7337692-0-4

Library of Congress Cataloging-in-Publication Data
Names: Dummel, Devin, 1983 – author.
Tile: One Life to Live / Devin Dummel
Description: Ingalls, Indiana: High Five Publishing, [2017]
Identifiers: LCCN 2019902304 I ISBN 9781733769204

If you enjoy this book, please tell a friend.

#1Life2Live

In Memory of H. Burton Fisher

A man who lived this life well!

When I finally grow up
I hope my life will in
some way resemble yours:

A devoted husband,
loving father and grandfather

passionate for Jesus, and
always willing to give everything away.

I will see you again my friend,
and when I do, I can't wait
to hear what you have to tell me.

"If you try to hang on to your life, you will lose it. But if you give up your life for my sake, you will save it."

-Matt 16v25

Table of Contents

Introduction

We may live in one of the most challenging times in history.

Every day we navigate cultural landmines, trying not to offend or upset the diverse group of people that we share this planet with.

Our culture is one that would rather highlight the things that separate than things that unite us. Everyone is hyper-focused on how they are not like "those" people; afraid to be associated with what disagrees with us. But in the middle of all of the division, we all share undeniable common ground.

We all have one life to live.

We can find division through gender, ethnicity, economic opportunity, political leaning, and religious views. We can debate back and forth our positions on core values and inalienable rights. We can disagree about raising children, the death penalty, and which came first - the chicken or the egg.

But unless you believe in reincarnation, there's one thing that we all have to agree on. Every person gets one life to live.

That's what unifies the world. We all get one shot at this thing we call life.

The amount of time we get is arbitrary. The specific situations and circumstances of our lives are largely out of our control.

But one thing that we can all embrace and understand is that no matter the hand we've been dealt, to the best of our ability we need to make this life count.

Because no one wants to waste their life, and this life is the only one we get.

At this moment, as far as I am aware, we've not discovered time travel. We can't go back and change the decisions we've made or alter the choices that have shaped our life.

As much as we would like to, we are not able to adjust our regrettable choices and redirect the course of our lives.

Whatever circumstance or situation you find yourself in as you read this book, frankly, is the situation you are in. You can't undo it. You can't take it back. You are where you are.

It often helps to understand how you got where you are or why you're currently there, but at this point, you can't change what's happened in the past; you can only change where things go from here.

And here's the thing I want you to know more than anything if there's one thing you read that I hope sticks with you, it's this: I believe that your life matters, and you only have one life to live.

If you've ever asked the question, "What am I living for?" then this book is for you.

If you've ever wondered what life is all about, then I am so glad you are reading this.

If you've had a moment where you wondered if life was worth it or asked yourself why you are here, then you are not alone.

I have been there myself. So many other people I know and have met over the years share the same sentiment.

Everyone wants their life to count, but most of us aren't sure of how to make that happen. In our best moments, we question if what we are doing is worth it, and in our worst moments we throw our hands up and wonder what's the point.

No one wants to waste their life. But how can you make sure your life really matters?

The great news is you don't have to wonder or wander very far. Your life matters and you are already living it. You have one life to live.

So, let's do this thing!

Let's take this journey together and discover what it looks like to live a life that really counts.

Prologue: Paper Airplanes

Every Friday in our house is "Daddy Day." What that means for our children, especially our young ones, is that Daddy doesn't go to work, and instead, they get to hang out with Dad all day long.

Although every "Daddy Day" is different, they all have some underlying principles that drive the decisions of the day. The first principle is pretty straightforward. It's this:

Keep the children alive.

This is the most important principle for "Daddy Day," and it will make more sense why this is even something that needs to be discussed after you hear the second principle.

But first and foremost, keep all children, and for that matter all other living things under your care, alive until mom returns home.

That is the most important priority of the day.

The second principle that dictates the activities of "Daddy Day" is:

What do you want to do? (This question is directed toward the child or children who are participating).

Whatever the answer to that question, that's what we try to do.

Cereal for dinner, sure - you got it, kid.

Wear pajamas all day. Sounds like a great decision.

Dress up like Spider-man and reenact the entire movie you just saw all day long - it's your world kid, I am just living in it.

Just to be clear, this is not an everyday strategy. It's just the core values of "Daddy Day." One day of the week. A sabbatical from normal living, if you will.

The final way I measure if "Daddy Day" has been a success is if we can say that we went to a store and returned without a toy.

If mom returns and we can say that we kept the kids alive, they had fun, and we didn't buy a new toy … that is a picture perfect "Daddy Day."

As you can imagine, when Friday rolls around you never know what to expect. One minute we're playing dress up and pretend, another minute we are coloring pictures to give to all of our friends.

On one particular "Daddy Day" I was at home with my youngest son, and he asked to get some paper out. He wanted to draw and practice writing his letters.

While he was busy being creative, I started folding a piece of paper. The more folds I made, the more his attention shifted from what he was doing to what I was working on. He asked, "Daddy, what are you doing?"

I gave him a typical daddy answer, "Just watch and see."

Once I finished, I could tell he kind of understood what it was but wasn't entirely sure. I said, "Buddy, it's a paper airplane. Do you want to play with it?" "Yes, Daddy!"

So, I handed him the plane, expecting him to climb to a high point like the couch or the table and then let it rip. But that's not what he did. Instead, he took the plane and began running around the room, making plane noises.

I'll be honest it was pretty cute, almost too cute.

But after he did this for a few minutes, I stopped him and said, "Honey, did you know that you're not really playing with it the right way? (According to my son's future therapist, I shouldn't have told him how to play, but I could tell he didn't understand how it was supposed to work). **(1)** You're missing out on the best part."

He climbed up in my lap, paper plane in hand, and asked me to show him. So, I took the plane and pointed it in the direction of the playroom. I pulled back, and I let it go.

His eyes lit up in amazement. He hopped down and chased after it as quick as he could. He brought it back to me and tried to do it himself.

Bless his heart, he tried, but he had never thrown a paper airplane before. He tried throwing it as hard as he could. Time and time again he tried but was unable to get the plane to fly.

"How do you do it, Daddy?"

"Well buddy, you hold it in your hand like this, then you pull back a little bit, and you just let it go – then the magic happens."

"How does it do that, daddy?" "I'm not sure buddy, that's just the way it works."

We played with that paper airplane for another fifteen minutes or so and then moved on to something else.

But because I like to know things, later that night once mom had returned home, with all the living things still alive, I looked up how a paper airplane works.

It's pretty scientific, but in basic terms, a paper airplane flies due to a delicate balance between gravity and the upward force of air acting on the plane.

That's how the magic of a paper airplane happens.

As I began writing this book, I thought this picture might be a helpful one to describe how the magic happens of finding the best life possible.

It's a delicate balance between the principles of God and the circumstances acting all around us.

The secret to making this life count isn't to overthink it.

Don't try to force it.

The trick is all about letting go and letting God lead you to the life that He has for you. We must learn how to pull back our control and let loose trusting God to help things fly.

May you be blessed by this book and encouraged to let everything go that is holding you back.

I hope you enjoy this journey as much or even more than my son and I enjoyed discovering paper airplanes on Daddy Day.

Chapter One:

Sinners and Saints

Blindsided

If I'm 100% honest … all I wanted to do was die.

It feels awful to say – but it's blatantly and transparently honest.

When "it" happened, I didn't want to live.

And I don't want to be weird or morbid or start things off on some dark and drab note, but truthfully, I sat in my car, my life spinning out of control, and I heard a voice that said, maybe it would be better if you weren't alive.

Playing the scenario out, the thought crossed my mind, "You could just unbuckle your seat belt and drive your car into a tree, and that would be the end of things."

It wasn't the last time I would have thoughts like that, but the genesis behind what happened on that day started a few months earlier.

My wife at the time and I were home for the holidays.

We were arguing again, something that seemed like our new normal.

This time we were arguing about why we didn't spend time with my parents when we were home visiting.

Things got pretty heated.

I was so mad I was shaking, so when we reached our destination, instead of going into her parent's house, where we were staying, I decided to swing by the store and pick up some brownie mix that we needed for a get together the next day.

I took my time and walked the aisles of the store steaming. I remember it like yesterday, trying to calm down, trying to regain my composure and return with brownie mix like a good husband would.

I was ready to apologize.

I was ready to move on, ready to go through the whole cycle again, if that's what I needed to do.

But when I pulled back in the driveway, my wife was waiting on the front steps and had my suitcase next to her.

When I asked her what was going on, she said … "I want a divorce."

I was blindsided. In hindsight, it felt like one of those moments on Survivor. (1) You know the ones, where once the votes have been read the only person who didn't know what was happening was the person whose name was etched on the parchment time and time again.

I suppose like those contestants; I probably should have seen it coming.

Truthfully, I had absolutely no clue.

The emotional whiplash I suffered caused me to spend the next two and a half months trying to figure out what happened and scrambling to figure out how to hold it all together.

She said she wanted to try and save us, but I'm pretty sure she already had her mind made up.

We tried counseling. However, I felt like I was the only willing participant.

So, two and a half months later, there I was sitting in that car finally grasping that my marriage was over and questioning if life was really worth living.

Looking back now, it all feels a little dramatic, but at the moment, I felt like I had lost everything.

It wasn't just my marriage.   This would affect my profession, how others would view me. Ultimately, it had me questioning my calling, what I believed God wanted me to do with my life.

At that moment I thought I had lost it all …

I felt like because of this divorce …

I wasn't a good man.

I wasn't a good husband.

And clearly, I wasn't fit to be a pastor.

Before all of this happened, I had felt like I belonged. I felt like I was "in" … but as I sat in that car, I imagined this wound would cost me everything.

The divorce would leave me on the outside, not able to belong or contribute to the community I valued so dearly.

I felt abandoned.

I felt lost.

I felt alone.

Sinners and Saints

Have you ever had a moment like that?

A moment when you felt like you lost everything - that gut-wrenching, sucker-punch, want to crawl in bed and never get out again, feeling?

Maybe for you, it's been more than just one of those moments, maybe you've had a few moments or seasons where, after the dust settled, you have questioned and wondered whether you were "in or out."

Have you had times where you were at the end of your rope?

If you are like me, when you are in the middle of those seasons - those times where you wondered if you belonged or were an outcast - you turn to a higher power.

Show of hands if you've bargained, blamed, or tried to bully God.

Can I get an amen if you've ever asked if God even cares about you or if you have ever thought He was working in everything and everywhere else except your life?

I think we've all had moments like that.

I'm pretty sure we've all been there.

We all know what it's like to feel like we are "on the outs" with God. It's lonely and terrible, especially when we aren't sure why we are going through it.

Sadly, because we have this struggle in our own lives, we are quick to identify and sometimes even point out when others appear "in" or "out" of good graces with God.

This whole cycle is sickening as many of us spend way too much time, energy, and effort evaluating and trying to discern who is "in" or who is "out" including ourselves.

The problem is we want clear lines.

We want black and white.

We want to know if you do *THESE* things and act *THIS* way then you are part of what God is doing; you're in.

And on the other side of the equation, we want to know that if someone's behavior is lacking, if it is less than Christ-like, then we are quick to point out that someone doesn't belong.

We all want to know who are the sinners and who are the saints.

We want those clear lines, but God doesn't always work that way …

or does He?

Three Pictures

Throughout this book, we are going to be spending our time taking a closer look at the letter that the Apostle Paul wrote to the believers at the church in Philippi.

This letter is incredible and in it, I believe, we will discover some of the secrets to living a life that counts.

If you want to make sure you don't waste your life, then the book of Philippians holds the key.

What makes this little letter unique is that it is the only letter we have in the Scriptures where Paul isn't trying to correct false teaching or correct bad behavior. **(2)**

The letter is basically Paul commending the followers of Jesus for living well and restating what it looks like to truly live the best life possible.

He starts the letter this way:

> *Paul and Timothy, servants of Christ Jesus,*
>
> *To all the saints in Christ Jesus at Philippi, together with the leaders and deacons:*
>
> *Grace and peace to you from God our Father and the Lord Jesus Christ. I thank my God every time I remember you …* (3)

As Paul opens his letter, you can tell how pleased he is with the people. When you first read this letter, you might get the impression that these people were "good church people."

You might believe that they were the "it crowd," they were the ones who had it all together.

You may believe that they never struggled or stumbled trying to figure out how to live.

My goodness, he starts off by calling them, saints!

He thanks God for them!

If only we could be so lucky to believe all the time that we were "in," but, if we are honest, many of us struggle. At the root of our spiritual struggle is one nagging question.

We wonder if God truly accepts us as we are.

If we had to choose between sinner and saint, if we had to check one of the boxes, more often than not we would check the sinner box.

When I was younger, I used to do this thing – when I was really hoping that something would work out for me.

- When I got my report card
- When I would call into a radio station trying to win a prize
- When I would ask a girl to go out over the phone

I would sit there and cross my fingers, thinking and sometimes whispering to myself, "Oh please, oh please, oh please."

I think many of us stand with this posture before God.

Arms out and fingers crossed, not really sure if we fit in the saints and desperately hoping we don't get lumped in with the sinners.

"Oh please, oh please, oh please."

Now at first glance, you would think that we don't have anything in common with the people that Paul is referring to as "saints" in Philippi. But what I believe is really interesting is that we know the origin story of this church.

These people aren't the nameless masses.

We know their names, and we know their stories.

We know where they came from and we can see that at one point these very saints that Paul was writing to in his letter were standing before God with fingers crossed saying, "Oh please, oh please, oh please, oh please.

Their origin stories can be found in Acts 16.

It's where we find three pictures of people who stood with their "fingers crossed."

Before we begin, it's important to know that Paul is on one of his missionary journeys.

He's traveling the known world at the time, trying to share the good news of Jesus and plant churches - not physical buildings, but groups of people who follow Jesus – everywhere he goes.

> *From Troas we put out to sea and sailed straight for Samothrance, and the next day on to Neapolis. From there we traveled to Philippi, a Roman colony and the leading city of that district of Macedonia. And we stayed there several days.*
>
> *On the Sabbath we went outside the city gate to the river, where we expected to find a place of prayer. We sat down and began to speak to the women who had gathered there.*

One of those listening was a woman named Lydia, a dealer in purple cloth from the city of Thyatira, who was a worshiper of God. The Lord opened her heart to respond to Paul's Message. When she and the members of her household were baptized, she invited us to her home. **(4)**

Here is our first picture of the beginnings of the Philippian church, and her name is Lydia.

Now there are some really interesting things about Lydia and the start of this church.

First, if you noticed, Philippi was a city of influence.

It was a cultural melting pot.

It was a major Roman city, and if you could be successful in Philippi, then you could be successful anywhere.

Based on the text, here's what we know about Lydia: She was a businesswoman – dealing in fabrics.

She was successful, *AND* she was living in Philippi. By today's standards, she might have been considered a fashionista and trend setter.

She was basically a CEO of her own fashion brand in one of the largest cities around.

The other phrase used to describe her is "God-fearer" and what this meant was that she had rejected the paganism and polytheism of the day.

Most people living in Phillipi would have worshipped any number of gods to bless their various endeavors. Lydia stood out because she didn't believe in many god-s she believed in one God.

But there is a problem for Lydia. As Paul and Timothy go looking for a synagogue or a place of worship, all they can find is a small gathering outside of the city.

Notice right away Lydia and her tribe are already outsiders. Lydia and the others who are seeking God don't have a way or place to encounter and learn about Him.

There is no church …

but they are about to become the church.

In a way, these women are gathering together doing the best that they can, trying to find and follow God with "fingers crossed" they are giving it the best they've got.

Seeking God, Lydia and her family become the first pillar of the Philippian church.

Let's take a look at the next picture:

Once when we were going to the place of prayer, we were met by a slave girl who had a spirit by which she predicted the future. She earned a great deal of money for her owners by fortune-telling. This girl followed Paul and the rest of us, shouting, "These men are servants of the Most High God, who are telling you the way to be saved."

She kept this up for many days. Finally, Paul became so troubled that he turned around and said to the spirit, "In the name of Jesus Christ I command you to come out of her!" At that moment the spirit left her. When the owners of the slave girl realized that their hope of making money was gone, they seized Paul and Silas and dragged them into the marketplace to face the authorities. **(5)**

The second picture isn't as glamorous as the first.

When you really understand what was happening it's not pretty. It may have been common in the ancient world, and far more common than it should be in our modern times.

But at the heart of this second picture is something most begin to shudder at when they encounter it: human trafficking, the exploitation of a minor.

There is a drastic contrast between Lydia and this slave girl. Two opposite ends of the socio-economic spectrum. Two different worlds existing inside the same area code.

While Lydia is seeking God, this slave girl is about as far away from God as you can be.

Lydia found new life through confession and baptism, and this girl found freedom and a new life through the deliverance only found through Christ.

Her deliverance and acceptance into a new community became the second pillar of the Philippian church.

The final picture begins as an extension of what happened to Paul and Silas after they delivered the young slave girl.

> *They brought Paul and Silas before the magistrates and said, "These men are Jews, and are throwing our city into an uproar by advocating customs unlawful for us Romans to accept and practice." The crowds joined in the attack against them, and the magistrates ordered them to be stripped and beaten.*
>
> *After they had been severely flogged, they were thrown into prison, and the jailer was commanded to guard them carefully. Upon receiving such orders, he put them in the inner cell and fastened their feet in stocks.*
>
> *About midnight Paul and Silas were praying and singing hymns to God, and the other prisoners were listening to them.*

Suddenly there was such a violent earthquake that the foundations of the prison were shaken. At once all the prison doors flew open, and everybody's chains came loose.

The jailer woke up, and when he saw the prison doors open, he drew his sword and was about to kill himself because he thought the prisoners had escaped.

But Paul shouted, "Don't harm yourself! We are all here!" The jailer called for the lights, rushed in and fell trembling before Paul and Silas. He then brought them out and asked, "Sirs, what must I do to be saved?" **(6)**

At that moment the jailer was at the end of his rope. He thought he had lost everything and was ready to end his life.

But God showed up and intervened in a miraculous way, and on that day, the Philippian jailer and his household were baptized and became part of the church at Philippi.

Three incredible stories of real people who encountered a living God that offered them a better life, a life that counted for something.

These stories are not the stories you would expect.

They aren't stories of the religious elite who have come to believe that Jesus is God's son. No, these stories are stories of people just like you and me.

People who are sometimes seeking …

people who are sometimes far off from God …

and even people who at one time or another have been at the end of their rope.

Fingers Crossed

Here's the thing. These pictures tell what I believe to be a beautiful story.

They tell the story of how God's grace extends to all of us. They tell the story that God is for all of us.

The truth is, I don't know where you are at.

I don't know your story. I'm not sitting across from you sharing a cup of coffee and hearing about your life's journey. I don't know your hardships.

I don't know if you've encountered God or walked away from Him.

My guess is that in these stories you probably have at least one point of connection. My hunch is that you probably know what it's like to be seeking something or someone bigger than yourself.

If I had to put money on it, I bet you at one time or another have been far off and distant from God.

I'm confident that many of those who read these pages have also had a moment or moments, even if they have only been in the silence of their hearts, where they have wondered if it was worth continuing.

I don't know where you are at.

But I know you are somewhere.

I don't know which of these stories you connect with the most. I don't know if you are like Lydia, seeking God regularly, but silently crossing your fingers.

I don't know if you're like the slave girl who has had some terrible things happen in your life or happen to you, and, if you are honest, you're reading this because someone recommended it, but in reality, you don't want anything to do with God.

Maybe you're sitting there, and you are so far from God, you're sitting there silently crossing your fingers hoping that no one asks what's really going on with you.

I don't know if you're like the jailer who is currently in a moment of crisis, not sure of what to do, not sure of how to react.

You're at the end of your rope, and maybe you've been where the jailer has been or where I have been, and you are wondering if life is even worth the effort anymore.

Maybe you're sitting there today – fingers crossed – hoping you can hold it all together and not fall into depression or despair.

I don't know where you are … but here's what I do know.

You are not alone.

If there is one thing we can learn from the beginnings of the Philippian church it is this – none of us have to live with fingers crossed, because God is always extending his grace to us.

In This Together

One of the greatest mistakes we can make in our spiritual life is our beginning point. Many of us believe that our spiritual life is simply about us. It's about how we interact with or understand the divine.

Because we start from a place about us, we often try to make judgments about if we are "in" or if we are "out."

We look around the room and try to decide who belongs, who are the sinners, and who are the saints.

But the truth is we are all in this life together. We are all trying to figure out what this life is all about. We are all sinners, hoping to be saints.

If it's true that we all have one life to live - the question we are hoping to answer at the end of this book is:

What does it look like to truly live?

No one wakes up in the morning and says, "You know what? I want to waste my life." Yet, it happens every day.

People miss the life that God has for them.

Most people who waste their life do so unknowingly and unwillingly. Days go by unnoticed. Decisions made unintentionally.

They go through life and let it happen to them, instead of discovering what it would take to live the best life possible.

That's why I am so thrilled you are reading this. You already are taking action. You already are deciding that you want God's best for you. You are being intentional by taking a step toward your best possible life.

But as we press forward together, let me share with you one very important truth:

If you want to truly live, you can't live with fingers crossed, hoping that if you do the right things and say the right things that you will "get in."

That posture never leads to a life well lived.

When we live with fingers crossed, our hands are occupied, tied up and contorted - unable to receive and really grasp the life that God has for us.

If you want to truly live, then it starts by unlocking your fingers and uncrossing your arms and letting go of that old posture.

It begins by getting ready to embrace the grace that God has extended to all of us.

No matter where you find yourself …

No matter the circumstance or situation …

You are not alone.

We are all in this together.

Chapter Two:

God at Work

Safety Coffins

In 1915, a 30-year-old woman from South Carolina named Essie Dunbar suffered what everyone believed to be a fatal attack of epilepsy.

After declaring her dead, doctors placed her body in a coffin and scheduled her funeral for the following day so that her sister, who lived out of town, would still be able to pay her respects.

Unfortunately, Essie's sister didn't travel fast enough and arrived only to see the last few scoops of dirt shoveled on top of the grave.

This didn't sit well with Dunbar's sister, who wanted to see Essie one last time. She immediately ordered that the body be exhumed. While that was a shocking development, no one expected what happened next; when the coffin lid was opened, to everyone's shock – Essie sat up and smiled at all around her.

This story sounds like it was crafted in a studio, designed to shock and to scare. But it's a true story even though it is unbelievable. What's even more incredible is that Essie Dunbar went on to live for another 47 years. **(1)**

In the days before sophisticated medical equipment could definitively determine when someone had passed from this world to the next, many people feared being buried alive.

This fear was so real that people developed strange contraptions to make sure that their loved ones weren't buried alive.

Of the many various inventions and designs, the most notable "safety coffin" was designed to ensure that, if someone was prematurely buried, they would have a way to communicate with the outside world to let them know that they were in fact still alive.

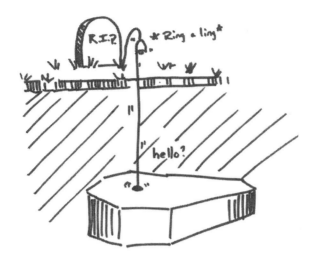

What a strange contraption. The thought of it alone is pretty creepy.

Can you imagine living in a world where you could bury your loved one, only to discover later in the week that they were still alive?

I don't know about you, but I sure am glad that we live in a technological age where you don't have to build special boxes just in case someone is simply "playing dead."

I'm glad we have ways to measure if someone is truly alive.

While the idea of waking up in a box six feet underground is terrifying, imagine the panic you would feel if you woke up to discover that you had missed out on the rest of your life.

This tragic reality is all too common, as many of us live without any intentionality.

Then one day, years down the line, we wake up and realize that we missed what mattered most. The only difference between us and the eerie fate of Essie Dunbar is we missed the step with the creepy box.

Unsure of Forever

Not long ago, my wife was reading a Bible story to our oldest son before putting him to bed. The topic of heaven came up and naturally, as most young boys are, he was very inquisitive.

My wife did her best to explain eschatology to a four-year-old but, in the end, my son did not find heaven to be a positive concept.

His exact words were, "I never want to go to heaven."

To a certain extent, I understand where he was coming from.

He has a pretty carefree life, and without having to deal with any heartache or heartbreak, he must believe this world is a pretty good one.

The people he loves live here. His house, his toys, and his friends are all here. Why on earth would he ever want to go to heaven?

So, when I got home, being the one who has two Bible degrees and who has worked with students and children in a faith context for fifteen years, I tried to set him straight on heaven.

I did my best to explain it to him, to help him understand how amazing it will be when we can spend forever with God. But what I was selling, he wasn't buying. He didn't want to give heaven a second thought. He was perfectly content with everything he has here and now.

Maybe that's where we find ourselves right now - perfectly content with all that we have here – enjoying the life we have.

Don't get me wrong. We believe in God, but at times we are unable to be 100% sure if He's really there, or if He is really all that invested in our lives.

We are unsure of what the future might bring, completely living for here and now.

What are You Living For

We all know what it means to live.

In the most basic sense, you are an expert at living, because you've been doing it your whole life.

But if you've ever been frustrated or felt restless in your existence, then you also know that there are seasons of life that are more "full of life" than others.

There's definitely a difference between "just barely living" and "living the best life possible."

So, the question we are getting at, the thing we are trying to do a deep dive on and really understand, is the question of:

What does it mean to really live?

How can we squeeze the most out of this life we have been given? How can we have the best life possible? How do we find a way out of depression, discontent and all the problems we face in our lives?

Why are we here? What is life all about? What is worth living for?

How can you and I live a life that really counts?

As I've mentioned before, I believe that you only have one life to live and that your life matters.

So let's continue to see what Paul had to say to the believers in Philippi about what it looked like to truly live.

We are going to pick up where we left off in the last chapter, at the beginning of Paul's letter.

He starts the letter this way:

I thank my God every time I remember you.
In all my prayers for all of you, I always pray with joy because
of your partnership in the gospel from the first day until
now, being confident of this, that he who began a good
work in you will carry it on to completion until the day of
Christ Jesus.

It is right for me to feel this way about all of you, since I have
you in my heart; for whether I am in chains or defending
and confirming the gospel, all of you share in God's grace
with me. God can testify how I long for all of you with the
affection of Christ Jesus. **(2)**

Writing over a decade later to the members of the church he
helped plant; you can hear the affection that Paul has for these
people. He has a partnership with them. They have supported
him, and he clearly believes that they are living and representing
Jesus well.

One important thing for us to note as we begin to read this letter is
that at the time of its authorship, Paul was in prison.

I don't know about you, but if I was in prison writing to those who
were my partners in ministry, I think I would have a different
attitude than Paul here.

Very candidly, I wouldn't spend a ton of time praising you and all
the good things that you are doing. I would instead be asking you
to start a *GoFundMe* page and bail me out.

I wouldn't want to spend another day locked up, not being able to continue the work that God put in front of me.

But there is something that Paul understands that we struggle to grasp, and he's already said it. Let's take a look at this again:

> *I am confident of this that He who began a good work in you will carry it on to completion.* **(3)**

You see, Paul recognized that God had already been at work in these peoples' lives. How did he know this? It was evident to him, after being in relationship with them for over a decade.

As they faithfully gathered together, God had been doing a "good work" in their lives, making them better people, helping them become more like Him.

Again, Paul makes it abundantly clear that he is confident that God isn't finished with them. He was confident because he was currently going through the same process.

He believed that God would continue to stretch them, grow them, and shape them into individuals and into a community that looked more and more like Christ.

Paul was confident that God was taking these people somewhere.

There was a destination where they were headed, and it was a place filled with more and more life.

Unfortunately, many of us say we believe what Paul is saying, but we don't actually live that way.

We say we believe that God is working to transform us, to make us more like Him, but in reality, we aren't focused on where God is ultimately taking us.

We can't focus on where He is taking us because we are too focused on what's happening right now.

We are satisfied with what we have here and now, making us unable to really grasp where God is trying to take us.

You see, one day you and I will stand before Jesus, and every choice we have made will produce something in us. It will produce one of two things: reward or regret. **(4)**

Those are the two options. Although we may not think of it in those terms now, as we stand before our Lord someday, each of our decisions will be measured and weighed.

If they have been wise, then they will have led to a reward in one way or another. But if they were unwise, then they will have been a waste, and ultimately leave us with a sense of regret.

Every choice we make, every ounce of time we invest, the relationships we have maintained or abandoned, everything will be put in front of us, and we will have to decide:

Did it move us in the right direction – was it a reward?

Or did it pull us further away from the life God had for us and, because of that truth, it's a regret.

I once heard Francis Chan use a similar illustration. I would like to borrow it to help make the point. **(5)**

Imagine for a moment that you are holding a long piece of string.

This string goes on and on forever. It never stops. When you follow the string with your eye, you see it touch the horizon, but you know that it goes well beyond that.

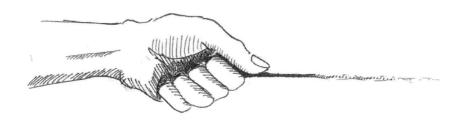

Now, picture in your mind that the end of the string that is in your hands is a different color than the rest of the string.

Let's say it's red. So, from your hands, going out about twelve inches, is red. Beyond that, the string changes color and then heads off as far as your eye can see.

Imagine that the section of string that is red is a timeline of your existence.

The portion of string in your hands is where your life began and where it ends is where your existence ends. As we've noted, it stretches on into eternity, just like your existence will.

Now take a closer look at just the red section of your string. It represents your life here on Earth.

Perhaps you could imagine each inch representing a different season of your life. The totality of red section of string represents all the choices you made and the type of person you have been during your lifetime here on this planet.

The rest of the string represents all of eternity somewhere else. In totality, this string, both sections, represent your entire existence.

What's helpful about this illustration and what's heart-breaking is that it exposes our inability to see the big picture.

Too many of us live with our focus solely on the red section of the string.

Because our focus is on the here and now, we often miss that true life - the best kind of life - can be found when we let go of the worries and concerns of today and instead live with the future in mind.

For example:

When you are focused on how you are desperate for certain people to like you.

When you can't see the future, you are devastated when things don't play out the way you wanted.

When you live with only today in mind, you get wrapped up and tied up in knots, unable to see the silver lining in your shattered dreams.

What's crazy to me is that we are so wrapped up in the here and now that we often jeopardize our future.

The Bible teaches that what happens in the "red section" of string (the part where we are on this earth)– the choices you and I make in this part - determine how we exist for millions and millions and millions of years, stretching on into forever.

If that's truly the case if the scriptures can be trusted, then why would I spend my time here trying to be as comfortable as possible, enjoying myself as much as I can, focused on all my wishes and dreams?

If what happens here and now determines what will happen for the rest of eternity, then there's only one way to describe what it's like to live focused on today.

It's CRAZY!

The challenging part is when you live with eternity in mind, some people will say you're stupid because your choice will affect how people view and treat you now.

But wouldn't it be much more stupid to treat yourself to all that you want now and then regret it for eternity?

You see the truth is we only get one life to live here on this earth and it can end at any second for any of us.

I don't want you to waste it.

I don't want you to screw it up.

I don't want you to be fooled.

I don't want you to spend your life trying to make the best "red string" when everything else is what hangs in the balance.

This brings us back to Paul, a man who understood this truth and was desperate to remind those who follow Jesus to keep it in mind.

His perspective was …

God has always and will always be working in and through your life.

He's been present in your past. He engages you here and now. And He will continue to move you toward His image in the future.

And here's the thing, all this work God does in your life – past, present, and future – isn't' done because he's trying to keep you from things. He has plans and hope for your future.

He's not trying to hold you back or limit you. He is trying to give you the best life!

He gives us direction and instruction out of His love for us. Like a Father who wants to protect His children, God tries to point us in the direction of life. He tries to help us steer clear of things that would hurt or hinder us.

Sometimes we miss that. Sometimes we don't understand it.

Like when I say to my boys, I don't want them dribbling the basketball in the driveway. My boys, focusing on the here and now, are upset.

Why won't I let them have fun? Why won't I let them work on their basketball skills?

Because they are so focused on themselves and what they want at that moment, they can't see the inherent danger in their desires.

I don't want to prevent them from getting better at basketball. I don't want to ruin their fun. I simply want to keep them alive.

As their father, I can see the big picture. I can see into the future. I can see that because they are new to dribbling a ball, and because we have an inclined driveway, that it's likely they will lose control of the ball at some point, and it will roll toward the street.

I also know that because they love their basketball, they will chase after it. And although I've told them thousands of times not to run into the street, they will continue to stay focused on what they desire and will follow it without paying attention.

I know that most drivers do their best to drive safely through neighborhoods. But I also know that there are times when a teenager is driving while talking to friends, or someone looks down at their phone for a split-second.

That's when tragedy can happen.

As their father, I can't afford that.

I can't live with that tragedy.

It's totally unacceptable.

I will do anything in my power to prevent that from happening.

So, when I tell them they can't dribble a basketball in the driveway, it isn't to steal life from them. It's to ensure that they get to experience all of life.

God is the same. He guides and directs us not wanting to keep life from us but wanting to ensure that we have the best life possible.

This is the perspective that I think we often forget about, and the perspective that God extends to us.

Too often we are tragically focused on ourselves and the smaller picture of life. But when we understand that there is so much more life beyond this experience, then we can understand and embrace a crucial truth: **God knows the absolute best life we can live.**

His motivation is for us to be able to truly live the best life possible. He created us and knows us. He designed everything about us. He wants the best for us. He placed hopes and dreams in us!

So how do we do that? How do we discover the way to live the best life possible?

If God has been and always will be active in our lives and we only get one shot at this life, how can we make sure that we don't miss out on truly living?

Well, let's check out how Paul closes the opening to his letter:

The Best Life

> *And this is my prayer: that your love may abound more and more in knowledge and depth of insight, so that you may be able to discern what is best and may be pure and shameless until the day of Christ.*

Remember Paul loved these people dearly. They were like family to him. His desire was that they would continue to grow and become more like Jesus, and in doing so they would be able to discern what was best.

Discern may be a word you are unfamiliar with but what it means is to perceive or recognize.

Paul's prayer is that we would recognize that the best way to live is God's way. I think when we hear that we would say yes, I agree God knows best.

But do you actually?

Because on a regular basis you make excuses for why God's word doesn't' apply to you. You heard somewhere that it's cultural or outdated, so you think much of it doesn't translate to modern times.

In some situations, you simply ignore it and say "Well, I know it says this is sin and it's harmful to me and to others, but I like the way it feels so I'm going to do it anyway."

Or what's even worse, some of you have accepted God's gift of grace and then say that. It doesn't matter how you live, because God's got you covered, so you don't have to try to live the right way anymore.

When I see that and hear that I think it's crazy.

It's great that God has you covered but why on earth would you want to live a life that is less than what He wants for you?

In so many ways, many of us have decided by our choices and actions that we don't actually believe that God knows best and we would rather navigate life on our own.

And here is where push comes to shove, here is where the rubber meets the road, here's where you find out if you actually believe what God says or if you're just going through the motions.

Because no one can decide for you how you will live.

Only you can make that choice.

So, you must decide if you will try to go your own way, make your own path and do life by yourself; or if you will trust that God knows the best life possible for you and choose to be obedient.

Sometimes obedience means saying, "God, I'm not sure why you say this or why it's supposed to be best for me, but because you say it - I will do it."

If you've come to believe that God knows the best life for you, you simply need to say: "God, show me where my life is out of line with the life you have for me and help me find the best way to bring my life into alignment."

Reward or Regret

Paul's prayer for the Philippians is a prayer that we should pray over ourselves, "God let us grow more and more into your image so that we may be able to perceive, recognize and discern how to truly live the best life possible." (7)

And when you do that - when you trust that He knows the absolute best for you –and allow Him to shape you closer to His image - you can trust Him not with just today's portion of the string, but the next section and the next section and the next.

The choice is up to you.

Will you live a life that leads to reward or will you live a life that ends in regret?

If you want to truly live, you can't live from fear and doubt. You must live from confidence in God.

When you let go of your control, and cling to Him then your life can change from good to great, from mediocre to amazing, or from dreadful to God's dream for you.

When you trust that He always knows the best way to live - you can let go of living for today and find true life by choosing His way to live.

Chapter Three:

To Live

Middle of a Storm

I remember delivering the hard news while trying to hold back tears. I stood in front of the congregation that Sunday to let them know that I would no longer be serving as their youth pastor.

My plan was to move home to try and save my marriage.

Most people were very gracious with me, telling me that they loved me and wished me the best. I could tell that for many of them, this was their loss as well.

They offered prayers and encouragement, and almost everyone said they hoped everything worked out.

Some tried to explain why things like this happen.

As if any of us are able to fully understand why hardship and tragedy happen.

Well-intentioned as they were, it helped less than they thought.

However, others felt the need to communicate something entirely different.

I remember getting a letter around that time from someone who had previously been frustrated with me and left the church.

In her letter, she informed me that my divorce was "God punishing me" and that God was using this pain as a tool to bring about repentance in my life.

Imagine yourself in my shoes, going through something so difficult I could barely function. Well, I bet you can guess how I took that letter … I couldn't throw it away fast enough.

While others weren't as strategic in their language, their comments hurt none the less:

- Everything happens for a reason

- It must have been in God's plan

- God must need you to experience this pain

I accepted their words politely but inside my skin was crawling. I was thinking … seriously, God made this happen?

I honestly thought that if God wanted to watch me lose everything I love, then maybe He wasn't a God worth loving.

I spent the next few months seriously battling depression and trying to cope with the pain.

Candidly, I spoke with God more often in this season than in the past. Often my conversations with God weren't polished or polite. They frequently ended with, "God, why don't you get off your ass and fix this!"

As I write this, it feels like I should feel bad for swearing or guilty that I ever let my faith get to that point.

But I don't feel guilty, and I'm not going to apologize.

It's what I prayed.

It was where I was at.

I was in the middle of a storm and couldn't see anything other than my hurt and pain.

Doubting God

I don't know if you've experienced incredible hurt and pain, but my guess is if you have, then you have been where I have been.

I think it's pretty normal to question the existence of God, to doubt the goodness of God when we are in the middle of life's storms.

When bad and hard things happen to us, it's natural to question if God is there.

There's this incredible book in the Bible about a man named Job.

As the story goes, Job is an incredible guy. He lives a godly life, and everything is going well for him. If there were a ranking system for all the humans on the planet, Job is at the top of the list. His life is perfect.

He is faithful, and his family is blessed.

But something changes and Job's picture-perfect life gets turned upside down. Bad things start to happen to Job and everything around him.

When I say "bad things" what I actually mean is terrible things. Tragedy strikes Job's life. It starts small, and then things get worse and worse and worse.

Things get so bad that Job's wife tells him that it's time to turn his back on his faith and to curse God.

She argues that a God who causes this (or who allows it) isn't a God that he should remain faithful to.

Sound familiar?

As word spreads that tragedy has struck Job's family, his support system kicks into gear. His closest friends show up. They intercede and intervene. And they start doing what a lot of friends do when these types of things start to happen.

They start trying to explain to Job why tragedy has found him.

They say things like:

Everything happens for a reason, and the tragic death of your family must have been in God's plan.

They even make the conclusion that Job must have done something to deserve this harsh punishment.

Again, sound familiar?

When we think of the ancient scriptures as irrelevant, disconnected, and inapplicable, we have made a tragic mistake.

Yes, Job's story is an ancient story. But his story is a human story.

His experience isn't too terribly different than ours.   If you haven't been Job, then you have at least seen a "Job"; someone who is a good person, who is living faithfully and then, out of nowhere, tragedy strikes.

It's inevitable …when bad things happen to good people, we struggle to understand what is happening.

We can't help but wonder if God is even there or if He even cares.

Chains for Christ

The good news for us is when we go through storms and even when we doubt God - we are not alone.

Like Job and the many who have come before us, we all have had moments where we have doubted or have been tempted to doubt God's presence in the midst of our trial or tragedy.

Paul has something to say about this topic in his letter to the Philippians, and it's crucial for us to understand his perspective.

But before we take a look at his words, I want you to recall the circumstances under which Paul is writing this letter.

This is a jailhouse correspondence. Paul has run into some trouble with the law, and I think this is something we often forget.

I don't know about you, but I think we often picture some of these authors or characters of the Bible as being people who didn't have a care in the world.

But Paul had his fair share of "Job" type moments.

In another letter he shared what his experience had been like, outlining the things he had to suffer through.

> *I have worked much harder, been in prison more frequently, been flogged more severely, and been exposed to death again and again.*
>
> *Five times I received from the Jews the forty lashes minus one. Three times I was beaten with rods, once I was pelted with stones, three times I was shipwrecked, I spent a night and a day in the open sea, I have been constantly on the move.*
>
> *I have been in danger from rivers, in danger from bandits, in danger from my fellow Jews, in danger from Gentiles; in danger in the city, in danger in the country, in danger at sea; and in danger from false believers.*
>
> *I have labored and toiled and have often gone without sleep; I have known hunger and thirst and have often gone without food; I have been cold and naked. Besides everything else, I face daily the pressure of my concern for all the churches.* **(1)**

That's quite the resume.

Paul's life was not an easy one. He experienced his fair share of struggles and storms.

So, as he is writing this letter to the Philippians encouraging them to live the best way possible, what advice does he have for navigating the storms?

Let's take a look:

> *Now I want you to know, brothers, that what has happened to me has really served to advance the gospel. As a result, it has become clear throughout the whole palace guard and to everyone else that I am in chains for Christ.* **(2)**

Notice Paul isn't blaming God for what happened. He isn't in chains BECAUSE of Christ … he is in chains FOR Christ.

Paul's perspective wasn't that God caused his hardship. It was his opinion that he went to prison not because God directed it, but because God was able to use it.

Let's follow his thinking further:

> *Because of my chains, most of the brothers in the Lord have been encouraged to speak the word of God more courageously and fearlessly. It is true that some preach Christ out of envy and rivalry, but others out of goodwill.*

The latter do so in love, knowing that I am put here for the defense of the gospel. The former preach Christ out of selfish ambition, not sincerely, supposing they can stir up trouble for me while I am in chains. **(3)**

So even while in chains, while drama and chaos surround Paul – some are responding in love – others are responding from envy and jealousy. But pay careful attention to what Paul says next:

But what does it matter? The important thing is that in every way, whether from false motive or true, Christ is preached. And because of this, I rejoice. **(4)**

Again, this ancient book is relevant for us right now! Paul's mindset is crucial for us to understand if we really want to live. If you want to have the best life possible, then listen up!

Paul believed that the circumstances were not important. What was important was that through all things, Christ is glorified.

If you want to live the life that God has for you, then you can't live holding onto the circumstances and challenges that you have faced or are facing. Your joy and your life are not decided by your current set of circumstances.

You have to let go and lean into the power of God to use your greatest tragedies for His glory and your good.

Remember, Paul is sitting in prison; his fate hangs in the balance.

He has no clue what's coming next. He's not sure if he has tomorrow.

He may not have another meal.

He is in the center of the storm, and there's no guarantee that he is going to make it out.

Now, listen to his heart:

> *I eagerly expect and hope that I will in no way be ashamed but will have sufficient courage so that now as always Christ will be exalted in my body, whether by life or by death.* **(5)**

Paul learned that the secret to truly living wasn't to focus on the circumstances but instead to focus on Christ.

Paul wasn't worried about the lightning strikes of life. He was focused and determined to live in such a way that God got the glory for his choices, behavior, and actions.

He couldn't control the storm, but he could control how he responded to it.

Paul believed that **if God allows you to go through it, then He will use it!**

Again, Paul didn't place his pain and suffering at God's feet.

He believed that God was so good, that when pain happened in his life, that there was no chance God would waste it.

If you are going through it, then God will use it for your good and, more importantly, for His glory.

Storms of Life

There are some things in your life that you have had literally no control over.

They have happened to you, without your permission, and you've just had to ride out the storm.

Other difficult situations you have some culpability in. You made decisions, and the consequences were less than what you desired. You had hoped to avoid some hardship and pain, but the reality is you could have done more to avoid it.

Perhaps you can think of a handful of difficult situations where you look back and think, "That was totally my fault."

All you had to do in these situations was make a different choice, and you would have avoided tons of hurt and pain.

When you look at the storms in your life, I don't know where you find yourself. Maybe you are one of the lucky ones who hasn't experienced much in the way of hardship.

Nothing crazy has happened to you.

Your greatest pain has come from losing a friendship, not being chosen to participate with a group or rejection from someone you had a crush on. To this point, you've managed to avoid the serious storms of life.

But I'm confident that many who will read this have already had their fair share of storms.

For some of you just when it felt like you had gotten out of a storm, the lightning seems to strike again.

- You've gone through a divorce
- You lost a loved one
- You were lied to
- Betrayed
- Abused
- Taken advantage of

I'm not sure what your storms have been like.

But I know what some of mine have been like and I've had moments where I wasn't sure if I could make it to the other side.

That may be where you're at right now.

Maybe you are questioning God, begging Him to get in the middle of this storm with you and pull you out to the other side.

I'm not sure what your relationship to the storms are.

What I have found is that far too often, the problem is we allow our focus to be on the circumstances instead of on Christ. We get distracted by the storm and what it's hurling at us, allowing the storm to get between us and God.

One of Jesus' closest friends experienced this very same thing. On one occasion, the disciples were together out in a boat when a storm began to pick up.

The waves buffeted their boat, and as fear began to grow in their hearts and minds, they saw what they believed to be a ghost – walking or floating above the waves. But when the "ghost" spoke, they recognized the familiar voice of their friend and teacher, Jesus.

He said:

> *"Take courage! It is I. Don't be afraid." "Lord, if it's you," Peter replied, "tell me to come to you on the water." "Come," he said. Then Peter got down out of the boat, walked on the water and came toward Jesus.* **(6)**

Peter stood in the middle of the storm. He literally walked on water. He was living the best life he could possibly live at the moment. But it didn't last long.

> *But when he saw the wind, he was afraid and, beginning to sink, cried out, "Lord, save me!"*

Immediately Jesus reached out his hand and caught him. "You of little faith," he said, "why did you doubt?" **(7)**

Peter allowed his circumstances to take his focus off of Jesus, and he began to sink. The same is true for us. When we hold onto your circumstance and situations instead of holding on to Jesus – the life God has for us begins to slip away.

I want to help you weather the storms and not lose the life that God has for you. So, I want to invite you to do something a little different right now.

Wherever you are - whatever your storms - I want you to take a minute and I want you to look at the next page.

Go ahead, take a peek and then read the information below:

Find the page with the lightning bolt and tear it out. Go ahead, use scissors or your bare hands and cut or tear out the bolt icon.

I want you to take a moment, and find a song. You can look it up online. It's called *"Praise You in This Storm"* by Casting Crowns. As you play this song, I want you to take the time to write on the icon provided.

Write down all the things that have you doubting or questioning God. Go ahead and do this now. And continue with this chapter once you've taken the time to complete this exercise.

Where ever you are, whatever storms you have been through, whatever you have written down - I want you to hear Paul's words:

For to me, to live is Christ and to die is gain. **(8)**

For Paul living was all about bringing glory to Christ.

All of life was worthwhile work.

Taking our circumstances and instead of holding onto them, releasing them and turning them to Christ - that is what truly living was all about.

The way Paul saw it …

One day, sometime in the future he would die.

He would spend eternity with Christ – and that would be the ultimate prize.

It was a win-win for Paul!

No matter what happened to him in the middle of prison, no matter what the result of his storm was - He would win. God would be glorified no matter what.

Paul's point was that to truly live you must have the right perspective.

You have to quit holding on and begin to let go and trust that God is always at work, even in the middle of your storms.

Earlier I shared this thought …

If God allows you to go through it, then He will use it.

It's a true statement, but not entirely so.

It's not complete.

Because God never has and never will force His will on us. So, a more proper way to understand this concept is like this:

If God allows you to go through it, then He will use it - if you allow Him to.

I think we know this to be true.

No matter the circumstances, we have a choice surrounding how we handle it, view it and react to it. Ultimately, you control whether or not the storms in your life are used for your good and God's glory.

Don't miss that. It's huge!

It's a concept that could change your life if you are willing to let go of the clichés attached to hardship and tragedy.

You are the one in control of your pain and its purpose.

You can't control the storm, but you can control how you respond.

You can control your perspective. You are in control of your future, no matter the circumstances you face.

Whatever Happens

Paul goes on to close this section of his letter by saying:

> *"Whatever happens, conduct yourselves in a manner worthy of the gospel of Christ."* **(9)**

What Paul means is - no matter what happens … no matter the circumstances that come our way – no matter the storms we face … we should live from the perspective that:

Our words …

Our conduct …

Our actions …

Would be worthy of the sacrifice that Jesus made for us.

Paul is saying, no matter if you are in chains, no matter if lightning strikes, continue to live in such a way that God is glorified.

Now take a moment to look at what you've written down.

Look at the words and the lightning strikes of your life.

These are the storms you have experienced. They are the doubts and the challenges you face because of the circumstances you have chosen to focus on.

As we close this section, I want to challenge you to quit focusing on your circumstances and begin to focus your life on Christ.

That's where true life can be found.

That's where purpose and passion can be discovered.

That's where impact and influence are cultivated.

That's where you become a catalyst for change in your culture.

That's where Jesus begins not just to change you, but to reach out to other people through you.

I invite you to leave behind the circumstances and the storms - lay them at the foot of the cross and turn your focus to Christ.

Decide right now that no matter the circumstances you face, you will live a life worthy of the Gospel of Christ.

Chapter Four:

Worthy
or
Worthless

Famous

Growing up I always wanted to be famous.

When I was young, we didn't have anything like Youtube. You couldn't create your own channel or gain fame for being the best at playing video games. Everyone didn't have a camera in their pocket that they could transform into internet magic.

For a young Hoosier boy, there was only one path to fame worth pursuing: becoming a professional basketball player.

I remember begging my dad for months to put a basketball court in our backyard. Looking back on it now, I don't think he really wanted to do it.

But kids have this special power to wear down the wills of those that love them most (trust me, I know this first hand from my kids), so my dad finally decided that he would make the investment and put a half court in our back yard.

In my teenage mind, my dad had just made the best investment of his life, because after I made it in the NBA, I could buy him a house and put whatever he wanted in the backyard.

Once the construction was finished, I played every day, rain or shine, during the school year and during the summer.

I can vividly remember after we finished shoveling the driveway in the winter, we would head out back and shovel the basketball court, so we could get some shots in when it was above thirty degrees.

We played basketball constantly. We had neighborhood games that would begin on Monday after school and finish on Friday. We would play to 100 or 500 just to make things more interesting.

If my friends weren't able to come over to play, I would go out and practice shots from different spots. And if I really got bored, I would invite my little brother to play with me.

All we did was play basketball.

It didn't matter who was there, what game we were playing, the weather or whatever else was going on, we were putting work in, having fun, and shooting hoops.

One thing I would do before I left the court was spend a few minutes practicing hitting the game-winning shot.

Tie score … clock winding down … Devin with the ball in his hands … 5….4….3…2…1 …

Buzzzzzzz …

I would picture that moment and dream of making it a reality.

I wanted to be famous.

A Worthy Life

As I got older, I realized that I was good at basketball, but I wasn't great. The truth was basketball would be a fun sport and hobby, but I wasn't going to become a famous basketball player.

But the drive to be someone to make a difference in the world never left me. I wanted to be someone who mattered, someone who shined. I wanted to be someone who made a difference in this world.

I think we can all connect with that idea. We all want our lives to matter.

No one wakes up in the morning saying, "You know what, I want to waste my life." That just doesn't happen.

When it's all said and done, and we are buried in the ground, or scattered somewhere, no one wants people to forget them.

Everyone wants to make sure that their life counted.

Not everyone wants to be famous, but everyone wants their life to mean something … but that's the tension, right?

Because we all want to live a life that matters, but we are very aware that every day people live lives that have little impact and hardly any significance.

So, the question for us becomes, if we want to live a life that matters, how do we do that?

In the last chapter, we saw how Paul encourages us to live a life that is worthy of the Gospel.

And that's great - that's what we should all strive to do.

Thank you for pointing that out, Paul … but how? What does it mean?

How do we live a life worthy of Jesus' sacrifice?

That seems like a tall order.

So, the questions we are left with are:

- What does it look like to live a life that really matters?

- How can we truly live a life that makes a difference?

Best Life Possible

Although the Philippian church was doing a good job of living out their faith, Paul wanted to reinforce what it looked like to live this way.

So, he continued to give them encouragement and direction, helping them, and hopefully us, answer the question of what a worthy life looks like.

"If you have any encouragement from being united with Christ, if any comfort from his love, if any fellowship in the Spirit, if any tenderness and compassion, then make my joy complete by being like-minded, having the same love, being one in spirit and purpose." (1)

In this passage, Paul is saying if you have experienced God and if Christ has made a difference in your life, then anyone who has experienced that reality should have a certain mindset.

If you would include yourself in that group of people who have experienced God and made Christ your savior, Lord, and boss, then Paul says you should be living out the same kind of love.

To put it more plainly: everyone who falls into this group should live differently than the world around them.

There should be a certain pattern to their lives that would look similar to each other and help identify them as Jesus followers.

Luckily for us, Paul goes on to tell us what that life looks like, so pay close attention:

"Do nothing out of selfish ambition or vain conceit, but in humility consider others better than yourselves. Each of you should look not only to your own interests but also to the interests of others." Your attitude should be the same as that of Christ Jesus" (2)

I wish we had time to just write a whole book on just those few verses. There's so much good stuff there that we could really unpack that for a while.

I don't know if you are a bullet point person or a list person, or a "write it on a post-it and keep it by your mirror" person, but what I want you to do is to start making a list of the things that identify what a life that is worthy of the gospel looks like.

So first a life that is worthy is:

1) A Humble Life.

What is humility?

Well, some people mistake humility as thinking lowly of yourself. They view it as being hard on yourself. While it may feel that way at times, the reality is humility means simply having an appropriate view of yourself.

Our culture tells us that we should live in such a way that we make everything about us.

When you take what our consumer culture sells us at face value, we are told to act as if the world revolved around us.

But when we step back and realize that God created us and loves us and has a plan for us, we quickly have to realize that the world doesn't focus on us.

It is focused on God and what He wants to do.

To be humble means to think rightly of ourselves; to know the part that we play in God's story and to, more importantly, know that the story is really about Him.

This is why Paul says – "*Do nothing out of selfish ambition or vain conceit.*" He's telling us that if we want to live a life that really matters and makes a difference then we can't make the mistake of trying to hijack God's story.

We can't make the story about us.

Everything we do needs to come from a place of humility.

The next thing Paul says we must do to live a life that is worthy is to make sure that we are …

2) Putting Others First.

Paul goes as far as to say that we should "*consider others better than ourselves.*" Why do you think he suggests this?

Think about that for a moment.

What happens when you look at everyone around you and instead of measuring yourself against them and trying to see who you are better than, you assume the best of them?

What shifts when we quit measuring ourselves against the room?

First, I think it makes the world a much better place, doesn't it?

When you view people at their best, you treat them the best, even if they don't seem deserving. When you aren't jockeying for social position, you release the potential tension.

When we think of others first and consider them better than ourselves, we remove all opportunities where we would have to remove our foot from our mouths or apologize for our actions and behaviors. It's another form of unconditional, sacrificial love.

It may not seem logical. But Paul doesn't advocate for human logic or rational. God's standard is different, and it goes beyond treating people well only when they have "earned it."

Again, Paul says, we should look out for other people's interests, not just our own.

The story is not about us.

The quickest way for us to live a worthless life is to live solely for ourselves.

We waste our lives when we focus our thoughts, energies, and attitudes solely on how they benefit ourselves.

Now, Paul was a master communicator and storyteller, and he had his entire experience at his disposal. He could have used all kinds of analogies and pictures to help communicate what this kind of life looks like, and I love what he does here next.

He wants us to get a clear picture of what our attitudes should be. He wants us to really be able to live, so he picks the best example he can think of.

He says:

> *"Your attitude should be the same as that of Christ Jesus: who, being in very nature God, did not consider equality with God something to be grasped, but made himself nothing, taking the very nature of a servant, being made in human likeness."* **(3)**

Paul is saying; you want to make the story about you ... well, Jesus? ... He was God; the story was actually about Him ...

but even He humbled himself.

He could have shown up and shown off.

He could have said, "I'm God! Do what I say!" Instead, He came and lived a life of service and sacrifice.

Paul keeps going:

> *"And being found in appearance as a man, he humbled himself and became obedient to death - even death on a cross!"* **(4)**

Through Christ's example, Paul wants us to make sure that we understand that living a life that is worthy of the gospel is a humble life, it is a life that puts others first, and it is a life that is lived out of ...

3) Obedience to God

Let's be honest; most of us struggle with this.

We want to believe in God and love God, but the part we wrestle and struggle with is being obedient to Him.

But here's the problem with that. When we live in such a way where we say, "God I believe in you, and God, I love you … but God, I would rather live my own way, what we are really saying is that the story isn't about God.

The story is about us.

We grow up with this desire to be known and to be appreciated – and our culture reinforces it – telling us to make our lives about us.

But if we believe that the Creator knows what's best for His creation, then we have to embrace that God indicates the best life we can live is a life where we aren't the focal point.

Jesus was once asked, *"Teacher – what's the greatest commandment?"*

Basically, someone asked Jesus what the most important thing in life was. Look at His response:

Jesus replied, "'Love the Lord your God with all your heart and with all your soul and with all your mind.' This is the first and greatest commandment. And the second is like it: 'Love your neighbor as yourself.' All the Law and the Prophets hang on these two commandments." (5)

Jesus said and modeled that a life of humility, service, and obedience to God is the best life we can possibly live.

Work Out

The example is before us … but the choice is up to you.

We may not have realized it until now, but Paul spells it out pretty clearly for us. Jesus' life is the example for us on how we can live a life that really matters.

Following His example is the only way that we can actually have what we want and what God wants for us. When we live for ourselves, we waste our life, but when we model our lives after Christ, we find significance, value, and impact at every point in the story.

That's the choice before you.

But no one can make you live that life. No one can force you to maximize the potential of your life you've been given.

Only you can choose if you will live a life that is worthy of the Gospel. Paul reminded the Philippian believers of this truth as well.

"Therefore, my dear friends, as you have always obeyed – not only in my presence, but now much more in my absence – continue to work out your salvation with fear and trembling, for it is God who works in you to will and to act according to his good purpose." **(6)**

Paul wanted them to remember that even though he was gone, they needed to continue to model their lives after Christ.

He wanted them to keep in mind that there was daily work to be done. Continue to WORK OUT your salvation.

When was the last time you worked out?

Did you go for a run or go lift in the gym? Were you at practice? Do you have a pattern of daily or weekly exercise?

What happens when you get a good work out?

You can feel it, right?

If you haven't worked out in a while, you can really feel it.

If it's been years, you'll probably feel it for a while.

Paul is saying, when we are living this way, when we are working out our faith, when we are trying to live lives that are counter-cultural, when the environment around us is telling us to make the story about us, but instead we try to make it about God and about serving others; when we try to be obedient …

It will be a workout.

We will feel it and sometimes it won't feel that great! When we push the boundaries of our faith, things won't always be smooth. They won't always be easy. And if we are doing it right, we will feel it at first.

But here's the great news: when you continue to stretch your faith and work out your spiritual muscles … you are not alone … look at the verse again.

> *"Therefore, my dear friends, as you have always obeyed – not only in my presence, but now much more in my absence – continue to work out your salvation with fear and trembling, for it is God who works in you to will and to act according to his good purpose."*

Paul says that while you work out … God works IN YOU. Remember He is always working for your good and His glory.

So, don't be surprised if living this way is difficult; it likely will be. But just because something is hard doesn't mean it's not worth it. Sometimes the hardest thing and the right thing are the same.

Light is Life

Paul ends this section of his letter with a picture. It's an image that reminds us of the potential impact a worthy life can make.

"Do everything without complaining or arguing, so that you may become blameless and pure, children of God without fault in a crooked and depraved generation in which you shine like stars in the universe as you hold out the word of life."

Even though living a faithful life in a broken world can be difficult, we should do so without complaint.

God is asking us to live like Jesus did, to see His example and model our lives after Him. He wants us to shine like He did. He wants us to be like the stars, shining brightly in the pitch black night sky.

We take for granted the stars.

We live in the iPhone generation, where we can press a button and let light shine from our fingertips. We often forget to appreciate simple technological advances like electricity and the lightbulb. But before those inventions, there was a simple truth, that we have neglected to remember.

Where there is no light … there is no life.

Plants need light to grow. Light strengthens our bones, boosts our mood, and helps heal our pain. Light is necessary for life.

There's no real benefit from the superficial light produced by our devices. If we need our bones strengthened or mood improved, we need more than artificial light. We need real light – the kind that only comes naturally from the sun.

The same is true in our spiritual lives. Superficial light can help you live a life, but the real light comes from God's Son. It's not artificial or man-made; it is genuine pure light. And it's only His light that helps us navigate the darkness.

Have you ever been somewhere and it's been pitch black, where there is absolutely no light at all? It's impossible to find your way or to avoid obstacles. It's actually difficult to do anything without the light.

Without light … we can not live.

Did you know that astronomy, the study of the stars, is one of the oldest sciences? It's also one of the oldest ways that humanity chose to navigate the world - through watching and tracking the stars.

As long as people have been on the earth, they have used the stars to help find their way in the darkness. Even certain animals use the stars to find their way nocturnally.

Paul implores us to shine like stars in this dark world while we "*hold out the word of life."*

Where there is no light – there is no life.

When we follow Jesus' example, when we live the way that He's called us to live, when we live the best life possible …
we are like stars who shine in the darkness and help others find their way to God.

Our lives become like the lighthouse on the shore helping others navigate to God safely.

The irony with this imagery has to do with something we have previously discussed.

Our culture implores us to shine but to a different end. We are goaded to make a name, to become famous, to get a star in our honor surrounded by cement somewhere.

But God invites us to a different life. When we choose to let go of living for ourselves and finding our name in the lights, we are able to truly shine His light.

When we let go of a selfish life and choose a selfless life, our lives shine brighter than any way before. They shine like stars in the universe, whose light echoes into eternity.

Where there is no light – there is no life.

So, shine brightly in the darkness ….

Let Christ's light shine through you and bring light everywhere you go. And never forget that where there is light … there is life.

Chapter Five:

This is Us

Depressed

I've always had a pretty outgoing personality.

I never really like hanging back, being quiet, or not participating. Over the years I've been pretty vocal, energetic, and often found myself in leadership roles.

When I was younger, I was extremely optimistic, always positive, almost annoyingly so. I was constantly looking for a way to spin every tough or bad situation into a positive one.

That's sort of my default mode. It's been that way for as long as I can remember. That's how God built me, that's how I am wired, and that's how you will typically find me.

But a few years ago, that wasn't the case.

During the season in question, I was working full time in a local church. I kept things together on the outside, but inside I wasn't doing so well.

Every week, people would see me, and I would be positive and encouraging and "have it all together." Then when I would go home, it would be completely different.

It was like I would flip a switch and go from positive – happy – energetic, to quiet - withdrawn and sad.

Full disclosure, during that season, nothing terrible had happened in my life. Sure, there were things that were difficult or hard. But nothing was extremely out of the ordinary … nothing except me.

Most days I would come home looking for a dark, quiet place to just zone out, which is a hard thing to do with two little kids around. It wasn't their fault. They had missed dad all day, and I was finally home, so they would do what two little boys naturally do.

They would turn me into a human jungle-gym. So I would wrestle and play, pretending to be happy on the outside, while things on the inside were pressing in on me and all I wanted to do was go watch Netflix.

It went on that way for months.

I'm not sure what my wife was thinking during that time. She noticed something was different. She prayed and prayed and prayed for me, of that I am sure.

But we didn't have any one-on-one hard conversations about what my problem was. She didn't get in my face and say, "What's the deal, dude?"

She was supportive, graceful, and consistent in how she cared for me.

She was incredible … I don't think I could have made it through that season without her.

Then one day, I mentally took stock of where things were for me, how dark and sad things constantly felt, how much I just wanted to be alone. And I realized that what I was experiencing must have been depression.

And it sucked.

Once I realized what was going on I knew I needed to get some help. So, I started talking more about how I was feeling. I quit trying to isolate and escape. I started being with people and I believe God started to bring me out of my depression.

You see, the root of my remedy is an ancient and well-tested truth:

we were never meant to be alone.

Belong

Deeply rooted inside all of us is the desire to belong.

It's a powerful desire that, when listened to, reminds us of our need for community. We were never designed to be self-sufficient.

Every way that God designed us communicates that we are intended for community.

We all feel the need to be known, loved and accepted. So, we go to great lengths, we struggle and wrestle, to find places where we feel like we fit in and belong.

We desire to connect so badly that we are willing to compromise what we believe is right and true. We will even do things we would never think to do as long as someone will give us their approval.

This is not what God had in mind.

The truth is, there are relationships that will keep you FROM the life God created you to live. They will pull you away from the best life possible. And we must do our best to navigate around those individuals.

But we are mistaken if we think we can do life on our own.

We were not created that way. We cannot live the best possible life on our own. If we want to truly live, we must find our people.

We must find people who are committed to a mission, who share a purpose, people who share the same fire and passion as we do.

As my favorite pastor and author Erwin McManus recently wrote, "When we find our people – life begins to come together in a way that it never could when you are on your own." (1)

Committed Community

Paul understood this, and in the community, at Philippi, he had found people who were committed to the mission and had the same fire and passion.

When you read through the book of Philippians, you learn about Timothy - a young man that Paul mentored and taught how to shepherd the church. Later, Paul would write Timothy multiple letters, giving instructions on how he personally could lead and live well.

Paul also shares about another man from Philippi - his name is :

Epaphroditus

Pretty strange name, not sure what his mom was thinking. But Epaphroditus was one of those people that Paul found who had shared his passion, and the church sent him to visit with Paul and to take their financial support for his mission.

Apparently on this trip, Epaphroditus got so sick he almost died.

But as Paul mentioned earlier, Epaphroditus lived a life worthy of the gospel and put his needs secondary to his mission. He was more concerned about spreading the good news of Jesus than his own well-being.

For Paul, Epaphroditus is a shining example of living the best life possible, so he tells the church in Phillipi to look after his dear friend:

> *"Welcome him in the Lord with great joy, and honor men like him, because he almost died for the work of Christ, risking his life to make up for the help you could not give me."* **(2)**

This is what the community is all about. This is how God designed it. If you want to look for a blueprint for what a community should look like, Paul is saying this is it. This is us.

This wasn't a shining example because it was flawless either. This wasn't some utopia where people didn't have disagreements. But Paul was quick to call out behavior that looked like the world, calling the brothers and sisters in Christ to let go of the ways of the world.

Take a look:

> *Euodia and Syntyche, I urge you to put aside your differences, agree, and work together in the Lord. Yes, Syzygus, loyal friend, I enlist you to please help these women.*
>
> *They, along with brother Clement and many others, have worked by my side to spread the good news of the gospel. They have their names recorded in the book of life.*
>
> *Most of all, friends, always rejoice in the Lord! I never tire of saying it: Rejoice!* (3)

Do you hear the connection to these people that Paul has? And what does he want these ladies to do?

He wants them to squash the beef.

He wants them to forgive and forget. He wants them to move forward. He wants them to be united.

Paul wanted them to understand that in Jesus, we don't need to find division. We should be unified and rejoice in who God is, what He has done, and what is yet to come.

God designed us for community, and He designed the community for us.

But what should this community look like?

What made the Philippian church a place where people like Timothy, Epaphroditus, Syzygus, Clement, and yes, even Euodia and Syntyche, could be a blessing to one another?

I will tell you what I think it is … I think it's two things

First, it was a community that was supported by accountability because …

1) An unaccountable life is a wasted life.

Paul gives us the example right here in the letter of calling these people out. He says, "Hey ladies, you have labored for the gospel together; what is more important than that?"

Whatever the issue is … let it go … in the big scheme of things, it's not really an issue.

It's great that we get this example because that's exactly what makes the church community different from other communities.

Because you are part of other communities, you have groups around your work, your sports, your kids' activities, your neighborhood, and friends.

Let me ask you, do any other those communities consistently hold you accountable to living the best life that God has for you?

My guess is they don't.

You see, God designed us for community. We need other people in our lives to hold us accountable, in a loving and gracious way, pointing out where we have gotten out of line with the best life possible.

Proverbs 27:17 says, *"As iron sharpens iron, so one man sharpens another."*

This is a powerful image we should grab ahold of. Every tool or weapon over time and use becomes dull. In order to stay sharp, and in order to remain useful, they must be sharpened with another blade.

If this is not done, they cannot be used properly. They can't be used to the best of their ability. They can't do what they were designed to do.

The same is true for you and me. No matter how good we are, the longer we try to do things on our own, the more likely we are to fail.

We can't do it by ourselves. There is no such thing as living the best possible life solo.

But when we allow others to sharpen us, that's when we find a better life.

James – Jesus' own brother – gave us these instructions:

> *"Confess your sins to each other and pray for each other so that you may be healed. The prayer of a righteous person is powerful and effective."* **(4)**

This might seem like a weird thing to do. I think we often think that confessing our sins is something that is between us and God.

But think about it … when you tell God the stuff you've done wrong … doesn't He already know?

Aren't you like, "Hey God, I really screwed up today, you will never believe it … and God's like … yep I know … I saw … I'm fully aware."

I'm not saying you shouldn't confess to God, because it's a healthy thing to do, but I want you to see why confessing to each other actually makes a lot of sense even though it can be difficult.

When we confess to each other, we are saying, "Hey, I don't want to be alone in my sin anymore. I've trying to navigate this stuff, but I can't do it by myself. Could you help me? Could you pray with me?"

And James is saying when we are able to let go of acting like we've got it all together and embrace the community God designed us for, that's when we can find healing.

I think it's crazy that some of us are dealing with some serious sin in our lives. We are struggling, and it's doing what sin does. It's wrecking our lives. By holding on to our sin, our lives aren't free to embrace the best life that God has for us.

But we refuse to tell anyone because we are too embarrassed, or we are worried what people will think … but the reality is confession brings accountability and accountability brings healing.

Being willing to be vulnerable and say "I need some help" is one of the first steps toward truly living.

Here's the critical thing: that can only happen when you are united in community.

When we live unaccountably, we live untethered, wasting our lives and learning things the hard way.

The second thing I see in the Philippian community is encouragement

Encouragement is crucial because …

2) A discouraged life is a distracted life.

A community that encourages one another is a community that is focused.

When we are discouraged, when we feel down about ourselves or our circumstances, where does our attention turn?

To ourselves, doesn't it?

But when the people around you are encouraging you and helping you see the best in yourself and a better future together, you can do unbelievable things. Even more, when you focus on others, making sure you are building them up, it reinforces you. It pours back into your cup.

Paul understood what united the community of Christ, what made it the body of Christ – was a mission.

That mission was and is to make sure that the world knows about Jesus - to make sure that we aren't distracted by other things.

Paul reminds us that,

> *Christ died for us so that, whether we are dead or alive when he returns, we can live with him forever. So encourage each other and build each other up.* (5)

No matter what we experience now, our community should be one built on encouraging one another, because we have something to celebrate and that news is worth sharing.

And the best way to share that news is by how this community actually lives.

Whatever is …

Paul closes this section of his letter by reminding us what we should look like not just as a community, but as individuals:

> *Finally, brothers and sisters, whatever is true, whatever is noble, whatever is right, whatever is pure, whatever is lovely, whatever is admirable – if anything is excellent or praiseworthy – think about such things.* **(6)**

Paul wants us to understand that we have a responsibility to one another. We are called to hold each other accountable and to encourage one another toward …

Whatever is true …

Whatever is noble …

Whatever is right …

Whatever is pure …

Whatever is lovely …

Whatever is admirable …

Whatever is excellent …

Whatever is praiseworthy.

These are the things that sharpen one another. These are the types of things that will unify us. These are the types of things that will bring YOU life!

The question is: will you focus on these things?

Will YOU allow others to hold YOU accountable to these things?

Will YOU encourage your brothers and sisters in these things?

I don't know what YOU will do … but I have to be honest; this is something that most communities are not very good at.

Whatever it Takes

We are good at watching what other people do. We are good about hearing the gossip. We're great at hearing what someone else said or did.

But we are not willing to do WHATEVER it takes to encourage each other to make better decisions.

We are not willing to RISK our friendships or our reputations to say – NO! That's not right; that's not what God wants! We have to be better. We have to shine a light in our dark world.

We aren't willing to stand out and sacrifice what other people think of us in order to have the life that God plans for us.

No! We all too often would much rather sit back and let life happen to us.

We would rather live distracted lives.

We would rather waste our time than be the community of people God has called us to be.

I'll be honest … I'm tired of it …

I'm tired of pretending … I'm tired of walking around acting like we are different when we look exactly like the world around us.

No wonder people don't take us seriously.

We don't take it seriously.

Here's the truth. We aren't shining the way God has called us to.

We aren't UNITED the way God calls us to be, and I think its time for that to change.

I wonder if you feel the way that I do? Are you tired of this? Are you fed up with just being like everyone else?

Are you hungry for the best type of life?

Do you want what is true … what is noble … what is pure .. what is lovely, what is admirable, what is excellent, what is praiseworthy?

Do you want those things?

Then will you do WHATEVER it takes?

Will you do whatever it takes to hold your brothers and sisters in Christ accountable from this day forward?

Are you able to make the commitment to encourage one another every chance you get? Can you set your mind today to make sure that you never say a negative thing about a brother or sister in Christ again?

Are you willing to do it?

I pray that you will …

I pray that from this moment on you will be united with the brothers and sisters in your community and that you will be different, that you would shine!

Earlier, I shared about my season of depression. Looking back on that time in my life, I am confident that one of the biggest contributors to my struggle was that I was so focused on navigating life alone.

I don't know if you've ever experienced anything like that. If you haven't, I pray that you won't. But I think to some extent we all try to go through life a little bit like I did.

We are trying to live a better life, and we act like we've got it together, but inside we are carrying a lot of things that no one else sees or knows about.

This could possibly be one of the biggest mistakes any of us (and most of us) could make.

So, I want to invite you to quit living out your faith alone.

I want to invite you into the life that God has for you, by letting go of those things that are holding you back.

It is my sincere belief that when you are able to let go of these faulty ideas and ways of living, then your arms are fully free to embrace a better way to live - God's way.

If you are ready to live the life God has called you to live in community, then today is the day to make a change.

Let go of what you've been carrying and embrace the community that God designed you for.

Reach out to someone you trust. Text them now. Call them. Let them know that you need them.

Once you let go of this absurd notion that you have to live life on your own, embracing the truth that you were made for community … that's when you can truly live.

Chapter Six:

Rubbish and Resurrection

Tipping the Scales

Throughout this book, we've been asking the question, "What does it look like to live the best life possible?" The question behind the question is, how can we tip the scales in our favor?

It's that deeper question that I think we really need to tackle.

We live from deep places, and when we aren't asking the right questions underneath our questions, things start to get a bit confusing.

So, what is the question underneath the question of, "How can we live the life that God intended for us to live?"

Perhaps a scene from one of my favorite tv comedies, *The Good Place,* can help us.

For those who have not seen the show, it depicts the events immediately following the death of the main character Eleanor Shellstrop, as she discovers that there is, in fact, an afterlife.

The scene below is the informational meeting presented to all who have recently found themselves in "the good place." **(1)**

> *"During your time on Earth, every one of your actions had a positive or negative value, depending on how much good or bad that action put into the universe.*

Every sandwich you ate - every time you bought a magazine, every single thing you did, had an effect that rippled out over time and ultimately created some amount of good or bad.

You know how some people pull into the breakdown lane when there's traffic? And they think to themselves, "Ah, who cares? No one's watching."

We were watching. Surprise!

Anyway, when your time on Earth has ended, we calculate the total value of your life using our perfectly accurate measuring system.

Only those with the very highest scores, the true cream of the crop, get to come here, to the Good Place.

What happens to everyone else, you ask? Don't worry about it. The point is, you are here because you lived one of the very best lives that could be lived …

So welcome to eternal happiness. Welcome to the Good Place. Sponsored by: otters holding hands while they sleep.

You know the way you feel when you see a picture of two otters holding hands? That's how you're gonna feel every day."

While I find the show to be hilarious, I tragically think many of us have a theology that was written for television.

What I mean by that is, we view our lives just like the previously described clip.

We live as if all of our actions are placed on opposite sides of a scale. All of the bad choices, actions, and behavior on one side, and all of the positive, good, life-giving choices or behaviors on the other.

While this makes for some great tv when you play out this system it doesn't line up with what the scriptures teach about how God views things.

Scoreboard

So, let's go ahead and play this scenario out: Imagine for a moment that you are holding two five gallon buckets.

The bucket in your left hand is labeled "bad," and the bucket in your right hand is labeled "good." The goal is to hold these buckets so that the top never dips below your waist.

For this illustration, imagine that all of your choices, both good and bad, carried with them some weight. Maybe picturing stones is a good way to think about it.

The more extreme the choice, the more extreme the weight, or the larger the stone.

Now what we want to do is determine if you are a good or bad person based on which way the scales tip.

Think of it like the first version of a scoreboard, except this scoreboard is going to determine your eternal destiny. No pressure.

With the buckets in your hand, think of some of the choices you've made in the last 24 hours.

Good or bad, place the appropriate weight in each bucket.

Now, think about your choices from yesterday. And tally all your actions from last week.

Don't forget about the thing you said when you stubbed your toe.

And I know it feels like it shouldn't count, but that thing you thought when your mother-in-law replied to your text? That counts too.

Remember no one is watching, so go ahead and add the stuff that you won't say to anyone because you are afraid they will disown you if they find out.

As you add more and more weight to your buckets, what begins to happen?

I'm not sure which way your scales tip, or which bucket drops below the line first, but one thing I am confident about is this … you are getting tired.

No one can hold all of that weight.

We weren't designed to hold the weight of all of our choices forever, carrying on in perpetuity.

The reality is that, as silly as this illustration seems, many of us live this very way.   AND IT'S EXHAUSTING!

Most of us believe that we are good people, but we also know those moments where we have been less than good.

So when we lay down at night, we put our heads on our pillows, and we rerun and replay everything in our minds-eye we are measuring if we were good or if we were something less than that.

We try to check our score and make sure we've done more good things than bad things in our life. We try to tip the scales in favor of being a "good person" more often than not.

And that's not the only way we try to measure our lives.

One of the reasons why we have to ask God what it means to truly live is because we have started defining life by so many other ways.

As a culture, we have said that you're living a life that matters if you have accomplishments and achievements. We strive for recognition and accolades to tell us if we have truly lived.

Some of us even choose to live in such a way that someone watching from the outside would believe that we live simply to accumulate more and more stuff.

And while those things are good things and they are options for how you can measure life, the question is what measure of life do they use?

Do they use God's standards or someone else's?

Skybala

When I think about those who have lived godly lives, the Apostle Paul is toward the top of the list.

Paul's letter to the Philippian church is significant because it is a letter written to a group of people who were actually doing pretty well living out their faith.

As he wrote them, Paul wanted to make sure that they weren't putting too much confidence in their choices and their actions.

Just because they were doing some things right didn't mean that they couldn't stray from the best life that God had for them.

Let's take a look at what he had to say in Philippians 3:

> *If anyone else thinks he has reasons to put confidence in the flesh. I have more: circumcised on the eighth day, of the people of Israel, of the tribe of Benjamin, a Hebrew of Hebrews; in regards to the law, a Pharisee, as for zeal, persecuting the church; as for legalistic righteousness, faultless.* **(2)**

If there was someone who checked all the boxes, someone who tipped the scales, someone who was the best of the best at following God … it was Paul.

9 times out of 10, he got it right. He was the best of the best.

But even though Paul could boast about his goodness, even though he could claim to be a good person, that's not the way Paul saw things.

Look at what he says next:

> *"But whatever was to my profit I now consider loss for the sake of Christ. What is more, I consider everything a loss compared to the surpassing greatness of knowing Christ Jesus my Lord, for whose sake I have lost all things."* **(3)**

Paul believes that all the good things he did, and everything that it got him, really was a loss.

As good as they were, when you totaled them up, they still paled in comparison to how great Jesus is.

Here is what Paul understood and believed:

Life is not about what you do. It's about what Christ has done.

The life that God has called us to live, the best type of life possible, isn't a life where we go around trying to do good things for good things' sake. It's not a life that acknowledges our own achievement or arrival.

No, it's a life that honors what Christ has done, a life that reflects and glorifies God!

It's a life that is lived out of appreciation and respect for the sacrifice that Jesus made.

Paul says that he doesn't DO good things to earn a reward. Take a look at what He says next.

> *I consider them rubbish, that I may gain Christ and be found in him.* **(4)**

Now we need to pause here because we're not British, and I can't recall the last time I've used the word "rubbish."

The translators of this verse are doing a little political linguistics here. I don't blame them. They are making it safe for the whole family. But I think it's important for us to see what Paul says.

Paul says that he considers all the good he's ever done in his life ….. "skybala." That's the Greek term he uses.

Everything is "skybala" compared to knowing Christ and placing his trust in what Christ has done.

This word is unique, and Paul only uses it once in his writings – right here in his letter to the Philippians.

The translators have chosen to use the word "rubbish," which is a fair translation. Garbage or refuse is an acceptable interpretation.

However, this word appears to have more force behind it and can also be interpreted another way …

Paul says that all his good works – all his efforts – all the moments in his life that fall in the positive category are "skybala" – they are this:

The point Paul is trying to make isn't that they are just a waste.

He's trying to communicate that the concept of placing our trust in what we have done or will do INSTEAD of Christ … is absolutely disgusting.

It's repulsive to him, and so he uses the strongest term he can find … "skybala."

To phrase it in a more modern vernacular - "The best of our best, without Jesus – looks like a pile of crap compared to Him." **(5)**

If everything else is negotiable, if everything else can be lost, if everything else if worthless – then what is worth living for?

Paul closes out this section of the letter by pointing us in the right direction:

> *"I want to know Christ and the power of his resurrection and the fellowship of sharing in his sufferings, becoming like him in his death, and so, somehow, to attain to the resurrection from the dead."* **(6)**

And this is what it's all about.

This is what life is about; it's not about what you do; it's about what Christ has done.

It's about, as Paul mentioned earlier in his letter, Jesus' willingness to humble Himself and be obedient, taking on the nature of a servant, living a perfect and exemplary life, and then taking our place by dying on the cross.

Our problem is that most of us have believed a lie, and it's a dangerous lie at that. And I'll be honest; we've believe this lie so much that you may cringe when I share the truth with you.

So brace yourself, because it may push against everything that our culture, your friends, and even your own emotions may try to say to you.

Here it is …

We believe that ultimately when you peel back the layers – that deep down – we are all good people.

But that is a lie … **we are not good people.**

"All have sinned and fallen short of the glory of God." **(7)**

We all deserve the punishment for our sin.

It's what we've earned.

Trust me; you do not want to be on the point system.

You do not want to be on the bucket method.

When we play those games, we lose every time.

You and I are not good people … we are broken people … we are sinful people in need of a savior.

Try all you can, do all the good that you might – it is impossible to earn your way back to an even position.

Because … *"The wages of sin is death."* **(8)**

No matter how hard you work, you still have to pay the price. And the price of our sin is death and separation from God. That's the only way sin is made right.

So, what Paul is saying here is that he realized this truth: that as "good" as he was by the world's standards, he wasn't really good at all.

So, he let go of pursuing righteousness and perfection and started to pursue Jesus instead, because Jesus is the only one to have overcome and conquered death.

For Paul, it quit being about what he could do on his own and became about the power of what Jesus had done through His resurrection.

Paul was willing to give everything up, to let go of his entire life, just to share in Jesus' resurrection!

Crossroads

If you've been tracking along through Paul's letter, perhaps this is where you find yourself, in a similar position as Paul, at a crossroad.

Literally, the CROSS roads …

Because when you come face to face with the crucified Christ, you have to make a decision.

You have to decide if you will continue to live for yourself – to DO what you DO to make yourself feel like a good person.

Or if you will quit trying to earn your salvation, and instead, like Paul, embrace the resurrection.

Will you come before the cross of Christ and admit that you are not a good person?

Are you willing to follow Jesus' example and humble yourself and be obedient, to die to yourself … so that you can find new life in Him?

Will you let go of the old way, so that you can embrace a new way to live?

The thing is … the choice is up to you.

It's not your parent's decision. It's not my decision. It' s not up to your friends, co-workers or even your pastor.

This isn't about what your spouse wants or about what looks good to other people.

It's not even about what you might feel like in some spiritual mountain top moment.

No, this is about you.

This is about you coming to a place where you can say, "I consider everything else – all of it – the good – the bad – the ugly – I consider it skybala, compared to knowing my Lord and Savior Jesus Christ."

Will you choose to make Him your savior or will you decide to do you?

Will you choose rubbish or will you choose the resurrection?

Paths

Even Paul, who shared this encouragement to his brothers and sisters, understood that his pursuit of the cross wasn't finished.

This wasn't another box he could check, but it was a path that he must continue to pursue.

Brothers, I do not consider myself yet to have taken hold of it. But one thing I do: Forgetting what is behind and straining toward what is ahead.

I press on toward the goal to win the prize for which God has called me heavenward in Christ Jesus. **(9)**

I don't know about you, but I love this language from Paul.

It's a comfort to us that even after we have chosen the resurrection, it's a process. God is still working to make us new.

Paul seems to say the key to this process is to make sure we don't dwell on the past.

Once again, don't focus on what you've done or what you failed to do; instead, focus on what God is doing and how He's calling you to take the next step forward. Let go of the past to move toward the life God wants you to live.

Paul closes this section by showing us that there are two different ways that we can choose to live:

> *Join with others in following my example, brothers, and take note of those who live according to the pattern we gave you.* **(10)**

He's saying, don't do this alone. Join together and follow the example set before you. Become part of the body and pursue Christ together.

What's the other option?

> *For, as I have often told you before and now say again even with tears, many live as enemies of the cross of Christ.*

Their destiny is destruction, their god is their stomach, and their glory is their shame. Their mind is on earthly things.

But our citizenship is in heaven. And we eagerly await a Savior from there, the Lord Jesus Christ. The reality is there are only two ways to live … you can live clinging to the cross, or you can live competing with it. (11)

Notice both options lead down paths. One path leads to destruction and the other toward our heavenly home.

It's not what you do that defines your life … it's about what Christ has done that can reframe your life.

Ultimately the choice is up to you …

How will you live?

Will you compete to find your life, or will you cling to the cross of Christ?

Which path will you choose?

Chapter Seven:

Fragrant Offerings

Old Spice

When I was younger, I spent quite a bit of time going on church trips.

Summer camps, weekend retreats, overnighters and lock-ins - you name it - I probably did it. I don't know if you've had any similar experiences, but if you have, maybe your group was like mine.

Our group was a close-knit group who loved to tease each other and have fun. One of the ways we did this on our trips and retreats was to pull pranks on each other.

One of my favorite ones was called "The Train." Here's how it worked: We would wait until someone was deep asleep; I mean like passed out and snoring loudly. Then we would get a couple of people, at least one who had a pillow, and another one who had one of these:

I bet you're starting to see where this is going.

So, you take everyone who is in on the prank and sneak into the person's room who was asleep, being very careful not to stir them.

Then slowly everyone would start making a chugging or a churning sound …

Chugga, chugga, chugga, chugga, chugga, chugga, chugga …

Then slowly the group gets a little louder and louder, and then just at the right second, as the person begins to stir, you blow the whistle …

TOOT! TOOT!

And as the person shot up, you hit them in the face with the pillow as hard as you can, and then quickly run out of the room.

Just thinking back to that prank still gives me an adrenaline rush.

Pranks were just one of the ways that we tried to have fun. We had all kinds of games that we came up with and played over and over and over again.

Probably my favorite game to play, of all time, I learned at church camp – it's called silent football.

My guess is that many of you haven't had the pleasure of playing this incredible game.

So, let me explain the basics of the game:

The idea is to follow the rules of the game and avoid getting points.

If you get three points, you have to do a dare.

The dares are decided by the group and usually are things you don't want to do. Some are goofy or funny, and some are just gross.

On one trip we were playing Silent Football, and there was a kid who was playing with us who had a reputation.

What I mean by that isn't that he was a bad kid. He was actually quite a nice kid. He was a little quirky, but for the most part, he was like the rest of us.

But he did have a reputation for being the smelly kid.

Now I'm not trying to make fun of him, because, let's be honest, we've all been the smelly kid before.   Especially at that age. Come to think of it; you might need to ask someone if you are the "smelly kid" right now.

We've all been there.

But here's what happened with Smelly Kid: as we were playing, he eventually got his third point and we dared him, or you could say forced him, to put on deodorant.

I don't recall exactly how he ended up with it, but before we knew it, Smelly Kid had his hands on some "Old Spice" and was totally focused on completing his dare.

Now you have to remember; this was a few years ago – long before any of their brilliant commercials.

You know, the ones that featured this guy: **(1)**

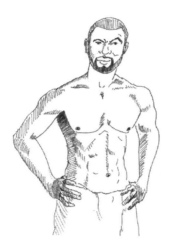

The Old Spice brand has since bounced back, but back when Smelly Kid got his third point in Silent Football; it was just an "old man's" deodorant.

The type of deodorant didn't matter, but it was extra special to us that he managed to put on some of our youth leader's deodorant.

But how amazing was that moment when Smelly Kid walked back into the room transformed into an entirely different person …

Then the heavens opened up, we were able to breathe again, and we affectionally renamed Smelly Kid, giving him the nickname – Old Spice …

And to this day, if any of us run into him, with affection we say –
"What's up, Old Spice?"

That moment changed things for that young man and for our
group, and, after that, there was no going back.

Continue

Throughout this book, we've been talking about what it looks like
to live the life that God has called us to live. We've discovered what
I believe to be a powerful truth: that God knows and shares with us
the best way to truly live.

We've looked at how when we let go of the things we are holding
onto; we begin to discover the life that God has for us.

When we let go of labels and quit worrying about being sinners or
saints, we find life.

When we let go of doing things our way and choose to embrace
God's way, we find life.

When we quit clinging to our circumstances and our chains and
instead embrace the power of the cross, we find life.

When we drop the false bill of goods our culture has sold us about
what a worthwhile life looks like and begin to value God's view over
our culture, we find life.

When we accept the truth that we were never meant to do life alone, and we need each other to navigate the storms we will encounter, we find life.

And when we let go of all the good we achieved and experienced, because we know that it pales in comparison to what Christ has done, that's when we've found life.

The secret to living a life that counts starts with letting go of the things we have taken hold of that aren't of God.

So, before you put this book down – the question is, what now?

What comes after this?

What does it look like to live a life worth living? Once you close this book and give it to a friend or take it to your local Half-Price Books; how do you continue to live?

How do you really live when you go back to your workplace, or back in the classroom?

How do you be who God made you to be in your home, or while you're running your kids from activity to activity?

Once we let go … how can we continue to live … and I don't mean just get by. I mean, really live the best life possible?

Fragrant Offering

I hope you've enjoyed looking deeper at the book of Philippians. It's a wonderful letter, a beautiful correspondence between Paul and his friends.

After you've read it, you truly get the sense that Paul is extremely proud of his friends. They are doing an incredible job living out their faith, so he wants to thank them and leave them with something they can take with them.

Don't forget, as he writes this he's in prison.

He is very aware that this might be the last time he gets to talk with them.

It's very possible this is the last chance he is able to encourage them and help them, so I think we should take a careful look at what he has to say, paying close attention to the message he wants to leave them with as he closes his letter.

> *How I praise the Lord that you are concerned about me again. I know you have always been concerned for me, but you didn't have the chance to help me. [11] Not that I was ever in need, for I have learned how to be content with whatever I have.[12] I know how to live on almost nothing or with everything. I have learned the secret of living in every situation, whether it is with a full stomach or empty, with plenty or little.* **(2)**

Paul is thankful for their support and their concern, and he wants to share something with them.

It's funny because I know this isn't what's happening, but as Paul writes this, I picture like an old grandpa type character who can barely speak above a whisper, and he's saying:

"Lean in here, sonny, I want to share something precious with you. I have a secret that has taken me a lifetime to learn and before I kick the bucket, I want to pass it on to you, so pay close attention."

So, as we lean in, listen to the secret that Paul wants to share with us about how to live ...

> For I can do everything through Christ, who gives me strength. **(3)**

Now before we unpack this, I know this is a super popular verse, especially with the athletes and companies trying to sell athletic gear.

I'm sure some of you have this verse written on your shoes or something like that, but just to be clear, Paul is not saying to them that if you're slow and vertically challenged, you can dunk if you ask Jesus enough.

Often, we just grab this verse apply it to any situation and say, "I can do anything with the power of Jesus."

While technically I agree, Jesus is God, and so He can do what He wants. I'm just not convinced that He wants to spend His time helping you dunk.

Look at what Paul said before. He said: He's learned to be content no matter the circumstances. He said he'd learned the secret to truly living no matter what was going on around him.

Don't miss this ….

He's saying if you want to live …

I mean really live … here is how you do it:

If you want real life, it is lived THROUGH Christ.

Paul is saying the secret to real life is when life quits being about you and begins to be all about Jesus.

You see when all your energy – all your emotion – all your effort – all your time is focused on you … it leaves no time for God.

When you spend every moment building your own kingdom, then there isn't any time lift to be a kingdom worker.

To really live a life that matters, a life that makes a difference, a life that is valuable, you have to start with embracing this truth that life is not about you.

This life, this world, this experience - you are not the star of it. You are not the boss, and at the end of the day, no matter what you do, you don't get a gold star.

Life is not about us. It's about God.

It's about His glory.

It's about what He is doing. It's about the story He is writing. It's about His love and His goodness.

It's about His grace and His mercy.

It's about how He died to show you how much you matter to Him and how much He loves you.

That's what this life is all about.

Now, here's the thing: when you get that concept, when you understand it – when you start not just to say "yes, I believe it and go through the motions" but when you say, yes, I believe it so much that I will live it" - that's when people will start to notice you.

That's when people will start to smell you.

You read that correctly.

You don't have to double back to double check. When you are living the life God has called you to live, people will smell you coming.

Listen to what Paul says about the Philippians, speaking of how they had lived out their faith

> *I have received full payment and have more than enough. I am amply supplied, now that I have received from Epaphroditus the gifts you sent. They are a fragrant offering, an acceptable sacrifice, pleasing to God.* **(4)**

Did you catch that …

They didn't make the story about them. They didn't focus on building up themselves. They didn't even get hung up on the change God had made in their lives.

They saw the Kingdom Work God had connected them to and they said, "You know what? The story is not about us; it's about God. How can we build His kingdom?"

Paul tells them that how they were living their life was a "fragrant offering." Other translations say, "pleasing aroma."

Did you know that God is in the fragrance business?

And it ain't no old spice …

Here's what Paul wants us to understand:

When others smell the love and grace of God on you, that's when you know you've found real life.

How do You Smell?

When God's spirit lives in you and your life is built around and geared toward kingdom work, you start to smell.

Your choices,

the way that you treat people,

how you handle difficult situations,

how you forgive,

how you choose courage …

these things become your offering.

Your very life begins to look like and smell like the love of God.

And that's what people are drawn to.

Want to know why they are drawn to it?

Because they rarely see something like it.

It's hard to find anyone in our culture who isn't in some way or another living for themselves.

So, when you see someone who will say, "I believe that God knows the best way to live and even when I don't understand it, even when I don't agree with it, and even when it's inconvenient, I am going to live His way", people can't get enough of it.

It's my prayer that as you continue in your faith, you would discover the kind of life that is a pleasing aroma to God.

It's my prayer that when people see you, interact with you, encounter you, they smell something different on you.

I pray they smell the love and grace of God.

Don't Stay There

As we finish up with the final pages, let me share something that I believe deep down in my bones.

What God stirs in your heart and your mind should never stay there. This is more than a theoretical exercise. It's more than expanding your knowledge and insight.

It's more than theology.

It's about taking what God is doing in your head and heart and moving it into your hands and feet. It's letting it travel to your lips and be the words you speak. It's allowing it to transform you from the inside out, so that not only do you know the best way to live but that you actually live it for yourself.

What God has done in you and is beginning to do through you ...
shouldn't just stay there.

The aroma shouldn't hang over one place, but it should travel with
you as you go - to your home, to your workplace, to the locker
room or the classroom.

In our crazy world, I hope you see that your life matters more than
ever. I pray that you know that you have the power to impact and
change people's lives every day, especially if you are willing to live a
life soaked in the love and grace of God.

Your life can make all the difference in the world.

But you have to choose if you want to truly live.

You have to decide, as you move forward from this moment, if you
want to go your own way or if you will choose to let Jesus be THE
WAY.

It's my prayer that you will join the rest of us who are fighting to live
the best kind of life.

I pray that you will find your community and your tribe who can
stand united together.

And I pray that you let your light shine brightly in the darkness,
following Jesus' lead every step of the way.

Because make no mistake about it … Jesus didn't claim to be an option to life. He didn't offer to be an alternative to the mainstream of his culture. He was clear when he said:

"I am the way, the truth, and the life." (5)

May you find the life you always wanted, a life that truly counts by letting go and trusting God in every area of your life.

Epilogue: Bring it into the Light

As I've been putting the final touches on this book, something weighs heavy on my heart.

In the community where I live over the past few weeks, we've had six students attempt suicide. Thankfully they were unsuccessful.

In a neighboring city, a young man about the same age tragically took his own life.

This morning I received a call of a young mother who tried to overdose.

I don't remember things ever being this heavy or this dark.

It feels like there is an assault happening at the very basic levels of what it means to be alive and to be human.

Honestly, I'm terrified to try to navigate this world with my own boys, knowing that there's the real possibility that they will experience and wrestle with something I am already all too familiar with – the desire to live.

There's something extremely difficult about broaching this subject with someone.

It's intimidating.

It's unnerving.

It's risky, or at least it feels that way.

We would rather dance around it, or gently ask if someone is doing okay, hoping against hope that they don't open Pandora's box by saying they don't want to live.

Because if they say something, we are not sure what we will say.

If they mention suicide or wanting it all to end, we aren't prepared to respond.

So, instead of asking we stay silent.

We don't ask what we don't want to know the answer to. We avoid the tension, and the mess, because maybe if we don't bring it up, whatever they are feeling will just go away.

We don't want to stir the pot, make things worse, or darken someone's day.

This might be our greatest mistake.

The Apostle Paul wrote to the Ephesians, that *"When all things are brought out to the light, then their true nature is clearly revealed."* (1)

I have found this to be true in both my personal and professional life. I have worked and wrestled through depression personally, and I have counseled many people pastorally.

What I have discovered is the most important step in dealing with the desire to live is to bring that thought out into the light.

If you are dealing with suicidal ideation or if you are struggling with the will to live, before you do anything else, tell someone about it. Talk to someone that you trust and respect.

Be honest.

Be vulnerable.

Be specific.

If you're someone who has a loved one share with you that they are struggling right now and not sure if they want to continue …

Listen.

Don't ignore them. Don't try to change the subject because it's uncomfortable. Don't tell them about rainbows and puppy dogs and how unicorns can solve all their problems.

Take them seriously.

Remind them that it's okay to not be okay.

Let them know that they can always talk to you and that you will always be there for them.

Remind them that their life is still worth living. And begin to find them the help that they need to overcome suicidal ideation.

If you or anyone you know is, considering suicide, please call the **Suicide Prevention Lifeline:**

1-800-273-8255

or text the **Crisis Text Line**

741-741

You only have one life to live.

It's never too late to use it well.

Please don't give up. Please don't stop fighting.

There are people who love you and will walk with you through whatever you need to walk through in order to get to the other side.

Whatever you do – bring it to the light! So that you can find your life once again.

So that you may truly live!

SPECIAL THANKS TO:

Leah for being always patient and ever understanding. You are one of the best examples I've seen of a life lived well. Thank you for always making your life count.

Declan & Dryden for being the inspiration to live my life well. I hope that someday you will read this and be proud of your dad because I know that I will forever be proud of each of you.

Nanci for the encouragement and insight. For being part of my tribe and believing that we can create whatever we put our minds to. I couldn't have done it without you! GSD

Pam for always being able to spot my mistakes, even when I would rather you overlook them. Thank you for graciously giving your time and gifts.

Samson for being a true "g." Your sketches make this book so much better, and your friendship does the same for my life.

Dennis & **Paula** thank you for loving me and empowering me all my life. I hope I've made you proud.

The Elders & Staff at Pendleton Christian Church for encouraging me to continue chasing down the dream, living my best life, and providing the grace and the space to work on my books.

And to the **many friends and mentors** who throughout my life have consistently and unapologetically demonstrated what a life worth living looks like – I thank you for following Jesus well!

NOTES:

Prologue: Paper Airplanes

1. I made a joke about my son talking to his Therapist one day. Just so we're clear, I'm 100% in favor of Therapists and the work they do. I'm more making a joke about my insufficiencies as a parent. Trust me I'm trying hard, but I'm sure I'm doing some damage that someone will need to sort out someday.

Chapter 1: Sinners and Saints

1. Survivor, which remains one of the greatest shows on television, should be part of your entertainment life. If it's not, then it's time to make a change.
2. Quote from Matt Chandler's Book "To Live is Christ to Die is Gain" (pg. 14) (2013)
3. Philippians 1v1-3
4. Acts 16v11-15
5. Acts 16v16-19
6. Acts 16v25-30

Chapter Two: God at Work

1. http://mentalfloss.com/article/54818/4-people-who-were-buried-alive-and-how-they-got-out
2. Philippians 1v3-8
3. Philippians 3v6
4. This is a powerful illustration that I first heard from Francis Chan.
5. https://www.youtube.com/watch?v=Bs33wVjQvJY

6. Philippians 1v9-10
7. Philippians 1v9-10

Chapter Three: To Live

1. 2 Corinthians 11v23-28
2. Philippians 1v12-13
3. Philippians 1v14-17
4. Philippians 1v18
5. Philippians 1v20
6. Philippians 1v21
7. Philippians 1v27

Chapter Four: Worthy or Worthless

1. Philippians 2v1-2
2. Philippians 2v3-5
3. Philippians 2v5-7
4. Philippians 2v8
5. Matthew 22v37-38
6. Matthew 14v27-29
7. Matthew 14v30-32
8. Philippians 2v12-13
9. Philippians 2v14-16a

Chapter Five: This is Us

1. Erwin McManus remains one of my favorite authors and communicators. I highly recommend his book, "*The Last Arrow:*

Save Nothing for the Next Life." This quote is taken from page 152. (2017)

2. Philippians 2v29-30
3. Philippians 4v2-4
4. James 5v16
5. 1st Thessalonians 5v11
6. Philippians 4v8

Chapter Six: Rubbish and Resurrection

1. https://www.youtube.com/watch?v=ut0ai4s4mjU
2. Philippians 3v4-6
3. Philippians 3v7-8
4. Philippians 3v8b
5. Probably my favorite quote from Matt Chandler's *"To Live is Christ to Die is Gain"* (pg 92) (2013).
6. Philippians 3v10
7. Romans 3v23
8. Romans 6v23
9. Philippians 3v13-14
10. Philippians 3v17
11. Philippians 3v18-20

Chapter Seven: Fragrant Offerings

1. https://www.youtube.com/watch?v=owGykVbfgUE
2. Philippians 4v10-12 NLT
3. Philippians 4v11
4. Philippians 4v18
5. John 14v6

Epilogue: Bring it into the Light

1. Ephesians 5:13 - Good News Translation

Have you ever wondered what it would be like to be famous?

"What if we were never meant
to sit on the throne of our lives?"

Available on Amazon.com

Made in the USA
Columbia, SC
20 June 2019